ELVIS PRESLEY

The Rise of Rock and Roll

Jc!

by
David Rubel

New Directions
The Millbrook Press
Brookfield, Connecticut

For Jesse

Produced in Association with Agincourt Press.
Interior Design: Tilman Reitzle

Photographs courtesy of: Michael Ochs Archives, Venice, CA: 6,
27, 36, 49, 53, 55, 62, 65, 71, 82, 85; AP/Wide World Photos: 10,
15 (bottom), 76; The Bettman Archive: 15 (top), 86.

Quotations on pages 14, 18, 20, 25, 30–31, 35, 37, 38, 40, 42, 47–48,
49, 79–80 from *Elvis: A Biography* by Jerry Hopkins.
Copyright © 1971 by Jerry Hopkins.

Cataloging-in-Publication Data

Rubel, David.
Elvis Presley: the rise of rock and roll.

100 p.; ill.: (New directions)
Bibliography: p.
Includes index.

Summary: A biography of the singer Elvis Presley, relating his
life to the rise of rock music and the social changes of the
1950s and 1960s.
1. Presley, Elvis, 1935-1977. 2. Singers—United States—
Biography. 3. Rock musicians. I. Title. II. Series.
B (92)
ISBN 1-878841-18-1

Contents

For their instructive guidance, both musical and syntactic, I would like to thank Michael Ackerman, Bill Kavaler, Eric Laursen, Peter Prescott, Howard Schless, and Robert Yampolsky.

Introduction

In the 1950s, Elvis Presley became the biggest rock and roll act of all time and a guiding light for the new teenage culture. After the advent of rock and roll, no one could ignore the teenage phenomenon. Elvis Presley played a major role in defining just what this word *teenager* would come to mean.

A significant influence on Presley was black music. Many of the most important American musical styles of the last century have been developed by blacks. Jazz, blues, soul, and rap music all express the unique situation of being black in a society dominated by whites. White teenagers wishing to reject their parents' culture have often been attracted to black music because of the powerful sense of rebellion it represents.

Elvis Presley was open to the influence of black music, especially the blues, which he was exposed to while growing up near a poor black neighborhood in East Tupelo, Mississippi. By combining blues, country, and a distinctive, faster beat, he was able to forge a new music that spoke specifically to white teenagers. And in moving his hips suggestively on stage, he represented a new sexual permissiveness. With his outrageously expensive lifestyle, he sent the message that teenagers should spend their money and have fun.

Years after his death Elvis still sells millions of records, people still watch his movies, and hundreds of thousands of people visit his gravesite every year. This book may help you understand why.

Eric Hirsch
Assistant Professor of Sociology
Providence College

The King in his prime.

1

The King Is Dead

"Come on, Presley, breathe! Breathe for me!" Dr. George Nichopoulos urged as the ambulance sped from Elvis's home at Graceland to the Baptist Memorial Hospital.[1] It took seven minutes at top speed for the ambulance to make the trip. All the way, Dr. Nichopolous and the paramedics worked to revive the King of Rock and Roll. They pounded on his chest and gave him mouth-to-mouth resuscitation. But it was no use.

August 16, 1977: Elvis Presley was dead at 42, in Memphis, Tennessee. He had been scheduled to give a concert the next night in Portland, Maine, but the show would have to be cancelled. Nobody could replace the King.

Word of Elvis's death spread as fast as the world's satellite network could carry it, faster even than a hot rod on a lonely road—or a rock and roll beat.

In Santiago, Chile, newspapers stopped their presses and radio stations gave up their regular programming for marathon tributes to "El Rey de Rock and Roll." Seven thousand miles away in Europe, Radio Luxembourg, the continent's most widely listened-to station, also switched over to nonstop Elvis, dropping even its commercials. "The King is dead," said John Lennon.[2]

Two days after Elvis died, *The Times* of London ran an appreciation of him on its editorial page. The conservative paper reported that the British Broadcasting Service, like so many other television and radio stations, had interrupted its programming to announce Elvis's death. It pointed out that this honor, usually reserved for the world's great leaders, was not inappropriate in Elvis's case. "While Presley himself was an indifferent singer and musician," the story ran, "performing for the most part mediocre songs, a poor actor and, it seems, a totally uninteresting person, the phenomenon which he became was of considerable social significance."[3]

No matter how hard you tried that week, you just couldn't get away from Elvis Presley. Even after his death, the man was still *hot*.

For three and a half hours on Wednesday, fans filed past his body to pay their last respects. Elvis's coffin was made out of seamless copper. Slick and clean, it sparkled.

Memphis's police chief estimated that as many as 80,000 fans jammed the sidewalks around Presley's Graceland mansion for ten blocks in either direction, cutting off two lanes of traffic. The average wait in the hot sun outside the gates was over five hours. The average viewing time was about two seconds. Even so, less than 30,000 mourners actually got in.

Worried about the disruptive potential of such a large and distraught crowd, the governor of Tennessee called in the National Guard. But that precaution proved to be unnecessary. Only two people were arrested. Hundreds fainted, however, and had to be treated on the Graceland lawn for grief and heat prostration. Several people fainted at the sight of Elvis's body and had to be carried out of the Graceland foyer where the coffin was on display. One man suffered a heart attack, and a pregnant woman went into labor.

It was quite a day. Florists all over Memphis sold out. The eleven Holiday Inns were totally booked. The local phone company reported that it couldn't handle all the long-distance calls. Avis, the rental car company, had no cars left. On Winchester Boulevard, the sign over the Pizza Hut had been changed to read "The King Still Live In Our Hearts." It seems that Pizza Hut had even run out of *s*'s.

People jetted into Memphis from everywhere, if they could get a flight. There were journalists from Japan, England, Sweden, and Australia—and housewives from Texas, Georgia, California, and Baltimore. One 54-year-old woman from Peoria, Illinois, had never been on a plane before. But "I just had to come," she told a *New York Times* reporter outside Graceland. "I always told [my husband] Ralph that if anything ever happened to Elvis, I'd be there."[4]

Another 40-year-old woman flew down with a friend from Massachusetts. "I was saving for a trip to Greece," she said, "[but] we both drew out every single cent we had to get here. My boyfriend said I should take the money and see a psychiatrist instead."[5] Even though Elvis's father, Vernon, compassionately extended the public viewing hours by a full ninety minutes, the Massachusetts woman was still outside when the Graceland gates were locked at 6:30 P.M.

In the meantime, the music was everywhere. Record stores sold out almost overnight; even the Christmas and gospel albums were gone. Said one record store owner, "It was as if some people thought that after he died, his records would no longer be available, which is hardly the case."[6] RCA, Elvis's record company, kept its Indianapolis plant running twenty-four hours a day to meet the demand, and still that wasn't enough. Although Elvis had already sold close to five hundred million records, there were some estimates that his death could sell a hundred million more.

Thursday was the day of the memorial service. Ann-Margret, who had starred with Elvis in *Viva Las Vegas*, came to pay her respects. So did John Wayne and Sammy Davis, Jr., and the governor of Tennessee. Chet Atkins, Burt Reynolds, James Brown, and Caroline Kennedy, daughter of the late president, also came. Frank Sinatra, O. J. Simpson, and Governor George Wallace of Alabama sent wreaths.

After an all-night vigil kept by an estimated one thousand people, Elvis's fans lined the entire four-mile route from Graceland to the Forest Hills Cemetery, sometimes five people deep. A stunning line of sixteen immaculate white Cadillacs followed the all-white hearse.

Presley's funeral motorcade.

Inside, Elvis's coffin was covered by a blanket of five hundred red rosebuds. Waiting at the cemetery were 3,116 different floral arrangements. Police motorcycles with flashing lights led the procession, and on-duty officers saluted as it passed.

The day before, callers had tied up White House phone lines demanding that President Jimmy Carter declare a national day of mourning. Instead, the President issued a statement. "Elvis Presley's death deprives our country of a part of itself," President Carter said. "His music and his personality . . . permanently changed the face of American popular culture . . . and he was a symbol to people the world over of the vitality, rebelliousness, and good humor of this country."[7]

Elvis was a rebel. Elvis was a punk. Elvis was the pink Cadillac he bought his mother with his first big record advance—just as fast and just as flashy. In the 1950s, he was everything that parents didn't like about teenagers and teenagers liked about themselves—Elvis was everything parents didn't understand. He was more than just a singer; he was a symbol.

A-WOP-BOP-A-LU-BOP A-WOP-BAM-BOOM! Little Richard said. But it was Elvis who *did* it. Before there was Little Richard, before there was Chuck Berry or Jerry Lee Lewis, before there were the Beatles—before there was even rock and roll, there was Elvis.

He came racing out of Memphis in 1954, pumping and driving like a steam locomotive about to blow a valve from all that pressure stoked up inside. Teenage girls screamed and fainted at the sight of him. When he appeared on the Ed Sullivan television show in 1956, the cameramen were ordered to show him only from the waist up, lest his swiveling hips and quaking knees shame everything that was decent and wholesome in America. Elvis was *dangerous* then.

He was an impossibly dynamic presence, an atom-powered star for the new atomic age. Elvis was always in motion: twitching hips, swinging arms, a pumping fist. He wore loud pink shirts, skintight pants, and his thick black hair greased back in a hairstyle called a ducktail. He had a throaty, suggestive voice, and he curled his lip when he sang as though he were sneering all the time.

When RCA Records bought Elvis's contract from Sun Records in 1955, RCA executives figured Elvis could make a lot of money for them in the very short term. Maybe, if Elvis had real staying power, his run at the top would last six months. Eight months, tops. At that time, a major record company such as RCA found it inconceivable that Presley's new style, this so-called rock and roll, could last. RCA's plan was to cash in and get out quick.

But the million-selling records just kept coming. With Elvis, everything was always excessive. For his Las Vegas shows, late in his life, he couldn't have just one rhinestone-studded costume; he had to have twenty. And Elvis couldn't have just one million-selling record—he had to have forty-five littering a career of more than twenty-three years.

From the beginning, rock and roll has always been about tension, and Elvis, too, embodied many tensions. He was a tough guy and also a mama's boy. He came from the country but lived in the city. He was white but he loved black music. Trapped by these dualities, unable to become one thing or the other, Elvis became the greatest rock and roller instead.

2

Sweet and Average

"This is the mystery of democracy," said the mayor of Tupelo, Mississippi, as he dedicated the boyhood home of Elvis Presley in 1979, "that its richest fruits spring up out of soils which no man has prepared and in circumstances where they are least expected."[1] He was quoting a speech that President Woodrow Wilson gave at the dedication of Abraham Lincoln's boyhood home.

On January 8, 1935, in a two-room house in East Tupelo, Gladys Smith Presley gave birth to twin sons. Tragically, the first, Jesse Garon, was stillborn. But the second, Elvis Aron, lived.

There is no telling what would have become of Elvis had Jesse lived. In that event, Elvis would not have been an only child, and Gladys would have had to share her love. But Jesse didn't live, and Gladys focused the love she had for two children on just one.

In 1935, East Tupelo was like a lot of other poor towns in the Mississippi Delta. The Great Depression was hard on the people, and most had either low-paying factory jobs or no job at all. Some—like Elvis's father, Vernon—occasionally found work as sharecroppers. A sharecropper farmed someone else's land in exchange for a share, usually half, of the resulting crop. But even farmers suffered during the Depression.

Gladys worked at the Tupelo Garment Company as a sewing machine operator. She had to be at work at six in the morning, and usually put in a twelve-hour day. She was paid by the piece, or according to the amount of sewing she did each day. A $13 weekly paycheck was a good one.

When Gladys became pregnant in 1934, however, she had to quit her job at the factory. As her friend, Faye Harris, remembered, it was "a hard pregnancy and she couldn't work, couldn't work at all."[2] Fortunately, though, Vernon had found a steady job as a milkman. He drove a truck for a dairy farmer named Orville S. Bean, delivering Bean's milk door-to-door in East Tupelo.

To make ends meet, Vernon and Gladys had been living with their in-laws, first the Smiths and then the Presleys. But now that they were starting a family of their own, they would need their own house. Vernon went to his boss for help, knowing that Orville Bean had helped other people. Bean helped Vernon Presley, too, building a house and then renting it to the family.

The house that Orville Bean built for the Presleys was typical for the poor families of East Tupelo. It was called a shotgun-style house. It had only two rooms; and not including the front porch, the entire house was 30 feet long and 15 feet wide. There was a small brick fireplace and a chimney built into the wall between the two square rooms.

The front door opened onto the bedroom; a door on the opposite wall led into the kitchen. Each room had a single electric outlet on the ceiling, but there was no running water. Water had to be fetched from the pump outside. Some distance away, there was an outhouse. Elvis would later joke that the entire house wasn't as large as his Graceland living room.

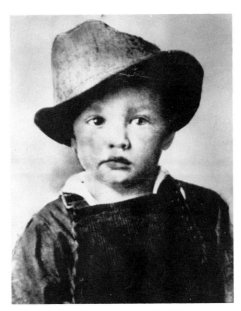

Elvis at age 2 or 3.

Elvis's birthplace in East Tupelo, Mississippi.

In East Tupelo, however, Elvis didn't spend much time inside. No one did. Instead, he played outside with his cousins and the other neighborhood children. Families in East Tupelo were large, and there were always a lot of kids around. Outside his neighborhood, though, Elvis was shy. He spent a lot of time with his mother. Every morning, Gladys walked him to the East Tupelo Consolidated School. Even years later, after the family had moved to Memphis, Gladys still walked Elvis to school. By some accounts, it wasn't until after Elvis's fifteenth birthday that he finally convinced his mother it was safe for him to walk to school by himself.

During all that time together, Gladys taught Elvis many things. For one, she taught him to be unfailingly polite: always to say "Ma'am" and "Sir," to stand whenever an adult entered the room, and never to interrupt or argue. Later, when Elvis would be attacked as vulgar and rude, his deferential and polite manner would do much to refute these claims.

Gladys also taught Elvis to believe in God. The First Assembly of God Church on Adams Street was just a block and a half away from the Presleys' house, and the family attended services there every Sunday and some Wednesdays as well.

To poor white congregations in the South, the message of the pentecostal church was a simple one: the last shall be first. With faith in God, that is, even the hardest of lives on earth could be redeemed. In return, churchgoers showed their faith by praying as passionately as possible. Members of the congregation would often cry out "Praise, God," or "Thank you, Lord," or "I love you, Lord."

The minister would also speak in tongues. He would close his eyes, fold his hands calmly in his lap, and begin speaking words that sounded like no language they had ever heard. To believers, this was direct communication with God. And always, there was singing.

Elvis heard his first music at the Assembly of God church. He and his family would join in with the choir's singing, which was something Elvis particularly enjoyed. Church music was called gospel music because its lyrics always referred to the teachings of the Bible.

Elvis learned a lot from gospel music. He learned how to sing, and he also learned how to perform. When one reporter asked Elvis where he learned how to wiggle on stage, Elvis said it was in church. "We used to go to these religious singin's all the time. There were these singers, perfectly fine singers, but nobody responded to them. Then there was the preachers and they cut up all over the place, jumpin' on the piano, movin' every which way. The audience liked 'em. I guess I learned from them."[3]

"When Elvis was just a little fellow," Gladys Presley would say, "he would slide off my lap, run down the aisle and scramble up to the platform of the church. He would stand looking up at the choir and try to sing with them. He was too little to know the words, of course, but he could carry the tune."[4]

Elvis and God were the two most important things in Gladys's life, and sometimes it was unclear which of the two received her greatest devotion. Gladys had such an overpowering love for her son that Elvis could not help but return it. As rock critic Nik Cohn later pointed out, Elvis "loved his mother to the point of ickiness."[5]

In general, though, Elvis was an unremarkable child. Besides his relatives, few people in Tupelo remembered him as a boy. One exception was Elvis's elementary school teacher, Mrs. J. C. Grimes. "He was a good student," Mrs. Grimes told one interviewer. "Sweet, that's the word. And average. Sweet and average."[6]

Mrs. Grimes remembered the day Elvis sang the song "Old Shep" in chapel: "Elvis sang it so sweetly," she said, "it liked to make me cry."[7] She had Elvis sing it again for the school's principal, and he was so impressed that he entered Elvis in the talent show at the annual Mississippi-Alabama Fair and Dairy Show, which was the local county fair.

Elvis was just 10 years old when he sang "Old Shep" at the fair, and he had to stand on a chair so that he could reach the microphone. But he won second prize anyway: $5 and free admission to all the rides.

Yet Mrs. Grimes's husband wasn't impressed at all. "I didn't think Elvis'd ever amount to anything," Clint Grimes said.[8]

"Old Shep," which Elvis would later record for his second RCA album, represented another strong musical influence on the young Presley: country-and-western music. Elvis heard gospel in church, but at home he listened to Nashville's "Grand Ole Opry" on the radio. Rock and roll had many ancestors but just two parents. Country music was its mother.

Country music was popular in the poor white South because it expressed both the secret hopes of the people and their secret fears. Particularly during the Depression, poor southerners had to stick together if any of them were to survive. Devotion to the community, like devotion to the congregation, was all-important. Yet country music singers stood outside the community. They were loners; they were outlaws. Their songs were filled with sin, sex, pleasure, and violence. Many died young, but that only enhanced their legends.

Through country music, people within the community could imagine another sort of life, a freer life outside, but still feel content with their lives inside. Eventually, both in life and in the songs, reality—in the form of a jealous husband or an angry sheriff—would catch up with the country singers. But the listeners on the inside were safe, and the unhappy endings justified their decision to stay inside.

Rock and roll's other parent was the Delta blues, also a music of the South. "It's the only place in the country I've ever been where you can actually drive down the highway at night, and if you listen, you hear music," Robbie Robertson of the rock group The Band once said. "I don't know if it's coming from the people or if it's coming from the air. [But] it lives, and it's rooted there."[9]

Just as country music was performed by and for whites, the blues was the music of southern blacks. It came from the slave songs and spirituals of the nineteenth century, but the music was timeless. Played almost exclusively on a single acoustic guitar, and sung by just one person, a blues song was always mournful and slow.

"You take the blues," bluesman Arthur (Big Boy) Crudup told an interviewer shortly before his death in 1974. "It means more than some people understand. A colored person ought to realize what the blues is because he's been having the blues all his life. He was born in the blues."[10]

Part of what the blues expressed was the sorrow of life in the segregated South. All through Elvis's childhood, blacks were kept apart from whites in the South. Blacks couldn't eat in whites-only restaurants, see a movie at a whites-only theater, or even drink from a whites-only water fountain. Until the famous Supreme Court decision in the case *Brown* v. *Board of Education* (1954), there were also separate public schools in many states for blacks and whites. The schools for whites were always better.

At the lowest levels of southern society, however, segregation had much less influence. In poor towns like East Tupelo, poor whites like the Presleys lived closer to and had more contact with blacks. Both groups were on the wrong side of the tracks.

As a result, Elvis heard quite a bit of the blues while he was growing up. And he liked it, despite the fact that his parents objected to it. "I dug the real lowdown Mississippi singers, mostly Big Bill Broonzy and Big Boy Crudup, although they would scold me at home for listening to them. 'Sinful music,' [they] said it was. Which never bothered me, I guess."[11]

When Elvis was 12, he wanted a bicycle. But his parents couldn't afford one, so they bought him a $12.95 guitar instead. His uncles, John Smith and Vester Presley, showed him a few chords, but the rest Elvis taught himself by listening to the radio and trying to copy the songs he heard, both country and blues. "I remember Elvis used to carry that old guitar around," said his cousin, Hershell Presley. "He loved that guitar. It didn't have but three strings on it most of the time, but he sure could beat the dickens out of it."[12]

Around the same time, Vernon Presley had a run of bad luck. A few years back, he had left the milk delivery job when there were no longer enough paying customers to support it. He had gone back to sharecropping, but that hadn't worked out either. So for a while, he had worked sorting lumber at the Leake and Goodlett Lumberyard in Tupelo.

But even with the lumberyard work, Vernon still hadn't made enough to support the family. They had lost their house and had moved several times. Finally, Vernon had decided to look for work elsewhere, so he had traveled a hundred miles northwest to Memphis, the nearest city. World War II was being fought at the time, and demand for defense supplies was high. Vernon had heard that quite a few factories in Memphis were hiring.

Well, Vernon had heard right. He had taken a job, coming home every weekend he could until the war ended. Then Vernon had moved back—for good, he thought—but things in Tupelo weren't much better for him than they had been before the war. By 1948, something clearly had to be done. "We were broke, man, broke, and we left Tupelo overnight," recalled Elvis, who was 13 at the time. "Dad packed all our belongings in boxes and put them on the top and in the trunk of a 1939 Plymouth. We just headed to Memphis. Things had to be better."[13]

They had to be, but they weren't. Memphis was a city of three hundred thousand people in 1948, but it couldn't house them all—at least not well. In Memphis, the Presleys were forced to live in even worse conditions than they had in East Tupelo. The first place they moved into was a one-room apartment in a large house at 572 Poplar

Avenue that had been divided up into sixteen depressing apartments. None of the apartments had kitchens or sinks, and the Presleys had to share a bathroom with three other families. The walls had holes, the heating was inadequate, and the electrical wiring was dangerous.

The Presleys were doing terribly. Vernon finally got a job at the United Paint Company, packing boxes for shipment, but he was paid only eighty-three cents an hour. In a good week, including five hours of overtime, he could make perhaps $38.50. In fact, the only good thing about Vernon's salary was that it was low enough for the Presleys to qualify for public housing. After a housing official visited them at Poplar Avenue, they were accepted into the Lauderdale Courts, a federally funded housing project near Vernon's work.

The Lauderdale Courts apartments were spare, and in a poor neighborhood, but they were clean and afford-able, with both kitchens and bathrooms. The Presleys couldn't ask for much more, and they certainly couldn't afford any more. They moved into their new home in May 1949, just as Elvis was finishing his first year at L. C. Humes High School.

3

The Memphis Blues Again

There were sixteen hundred students at Humes High, which was more than the entire population of East Tupelo. It was easy for someone as shy as Elvis to remain unnoticed. He made a few friends at the Lauderdale Courts, but most of his classmates at Humes later admitted that they had little more than hazy memories of a teenage boy wearing loud pink shirts and long hair greased back in a ducktail. All schools have their loners, reclusive students whom it seems no one knows, and Elvis was surely one. But even then he had an eye for flash.

For a teenager like Elvis, the decade of the 1950s was a brave new world. In fact, before World War II, the concept of the teenager did not even exist. You were a child, and then you were an adult. There was no stage in between. Before the war, most people in East Tupelo and Memphis got married, took a job, and had children, all before the age of 18.

After the war, everything changed. With the Depression finally over, America entered its greatest period of prosperity. It was being called the American Century, and nearly every American would soon share in its success, even the Presleys.

When the family moved into the Lauderdale Courts in 1949, Vernon's income was estimated by the public housing agency at $2,080 a year. This was well under the

$3,000 maximum income for families to qualify for public housing. But it soon began to creep up, from a $38.50 weekly salary in 1949 to $48.50 in 1951 and $53.22 in 1952.

Because jobs at this time were plentiful and generally well-paying, there was no longer such a rush for children to leave home or to find work to help support the family. Instead, the postwar prosperity led to more leisure time for people, and children didn't have to grow up so fast.

There was never any question, for instance, of Elvis dropping out of school. Vernon and Gladys knew well that the highest-paying jobs demanded ever more training, and that Elvis would get nowhere without a high school degree.

They couldn't give their son much of an allowance, of course, but mowing lawns was only one way the young Elvis found to put some money in his pocket. And money in a teenager's pocket was important. Some people have called the remarkable social changes of the fifties and sixties the "rock and roll revolution." But the first principle of that revolution had nothing to do with music. Instead, it was that kids have money.

In America, if you have money and you want to buy something, you don't have to count to ten before some enterprising businessperson will find a way to sell it to you. If kids have money, then people will sell the things that kids want to buy.

Also, teenagers have a particular kind of money. Most adults have to pay for rent, electricity, taxes, food, and so on, out of the money they earn. The money that's left over after paying for all the necessities of life is each person's disposable income. Disposable income is the extra money people spend on whatever they want—movies, records, fancy clothing. For most adults, this is only a small portion of the money they make; but for teenagers who live at home, almost all income is disposable income.

Although a fifties teenager such as Elvis may not have had much money, just an allowance or paper-route salary, imagine all of the millions of teenagers in the country taken together as a group. Together, they had quite a lot of money.

"I remember one time we were going to rent a truck for a hayride," a high school friend of Elvis recalled. "We all chipped in fifty cents apiece but we were a little short. So Elvis went down to the record store . . . and made an announcement that we were having a hayride and we had a truck outside. Pretty soon we had a truck full and enough money to pay for it."[1]

But having money wasn't the postwar teenagers' only distinguishing trait. They also wanted to be different from their parents, who were "square" and didn't always understand what was going on in their children's lives. Just as they do today, and probably will forever, teenagers wanted a separate identity. They wanted to choose their own clothes, listen to their own music, and even speak their own language. During the fifties, it wasn't the adults who said things like "Crazy, man, crazy" and "See you later, alligator."

In their effort to be different, the teenagers of the fifties developed a subculture. In America, there is one main culture. It is the culture of fast food and Levis and "The Love Boat." But America also has subcultures. A subculture is a smaller culture, just as a subset is part of a larger set. But a subculture usually stands against the mainstream culture, while struggling to survive within it.

In the fifties, black culture was a subculture. Denied for so many years inclusion in the mainstream, blacks in America developed their own culture instead. Over the years, black subcultures have embraced many symbols— jazz clubs, African clothing, razor haircuts, and the blues. The unmistakable Afro hair styles of the sixties, for example, were intended to show pride in the differences between black culture and the white mainstream.

Teenagers have often had similar feelings. They've wanted a separate identity, too, which is why the most important and influential teenage styles have always caused such uproar among parents. It's also why white teenage subcultures have borrowed so heavily from black culture. Throughout American history, blacks— merely because of their color—have been kept outside the mainstream. For white teenagers, the conclusion has been a very simple one: If you want to be different, be like blacks.

White teenagers couldn't become black, of course, but they could talk like blacks and dress like blacks and listen to black music like jazz and the blues. In the early fifties, white teenagers like Elvis were especially drawn to the fast, electric, citified form of the blues that was becoming very popular in Memphis and farther north in Chicago. Because of its loud, pulsating beat, the music was known as rhythm and blues, or R&B.

In Memphis, Elvis listened to Jackie Brenston's "Rocket 88," the Dominoes' "Sixty Minute Man," Hank Ballard's "Work With Me Annie," and Big Joe Turner's "Shake, Rattle and Roll." Elvis also liked Billy Eckstine and the Ink Spots. These were all black singers and black bands.

The black music scene in Memphis, which centered around Beale Street, was at its height when Elvis was a teenager in the early fifties. Howlin' Wolf, who would later become one of the most famous of the Chicago rhythm-and-bluesmen, was still living in Memphis and broadcasting with Sonny Boy Williamson out of radio station KWEM just across the Mississippi River in West Memphis, Arkansas. Sometimes the Wolf spun records; sometimes he played right into the mike. In Memphis proper, blues legends B. B. King and Rufus Thomas were doing the same thing over at WDIA.

B. B. King

Known as "the mother station of the Negroes," WDIA was the first black-operated radio station in the South. It played music by blacks and for blacks, but young whites like Elvis listened, too, because black music was the most exciting music around.

It's difficult to overemphasize the importance of radio in the spread of black music to white audiences. The South of the 1950s was a strictly segregated society. Blacks were not allowed to interact with whites at all, especially white children, and their music was thought by country- and gospel-loving adults to be sinful. But teenagers disagreed, and it was impossible to segregate the airwaves.

Radio delivered an entirely new kind of freedom. For Elvis and other teenagers like him, a radio was a lifeline. There wasn't much rhythm and blues in Hibbing, Minnesota, for instance, where Bob Dylan grew up. But there was a radio, and the young Dylan spent many late-night hours listening to B. B. King and Howlin' Wolf blues records on an AM station out of Little Rock, Arkansas.

For John Lennon, too, radio was very important. Lennon grew up in Liverpool, where there wasn't much R & B either. But John had a radio and late at night he'd listen under the covers to European radio stations beaming early Elvis records over the English Channel. The signal faded in and out like a secret code being sent to an occupied country, but the message got through well enough.

Back in Memphis, on Beale Street, however, Elvis was right in the heart of the music, and he liked it that way. He especially liked hanging around all the black bluesmen.

"I knew Elvis before he was popular," B. B. King remembered. "He used to come around and be around us a lot. There was a place we used to go and hang out at on Beale Street. People had like pawnshops there, and a lot of us used to hang out in certain of these places, and this was where I met him."[2]

But it was the movies that most captured Elvis's imagination. In the fall of 1950, the 15-year-old high school sophomore got himself a job after school working as an usher at the Loew's State Theater in downtown Memphis. He worked from five to ten each night and made $12.75 a week. Then he spent a lot of that money at movie theaters just like the Loew's State. One of his regular haunts in the Lauderdale Courts neighborhood was the Suzore No. 2 movie theater, where he would spend most weekend nights watching films starring Tony Curtis and Marlon Brando. Sitting through countless double features, Elvis daydreamed about one day seeing himself up on the screen.

Like so many other things, Elvis got his hairstyle from the movies. Elvis's favorite star, Tony Curtis, used to wear his black hair greased and combed back. From behind, his hair looked like the tail feathers of a duck, so the style was called a ducktail.

It was from Marlon Brando, however, that Elvis got his sneer. Of all the teen rebel movies that lit up movie screens for the next twenty years, *The Wild One* (1951) was the first and the best. Starring Brando as Johnny, the potentially violent leader of an obviously violent motorcycle gang, *The Wild One* was on one level about a gang of juvenile delinquents taking over a small town. On another, teenage level, it was about Brando's brooding, disaffected struggle to find something that was worth believing in.

"What are you rebelling against, Johnny?" a local girl asks Brando's character. Brando looks at her casually. Always calm. Always cool. "Whattaya got?" he says.

Elvis also spent a lot of money on clothes. Loud clothes. Special clothes. *Different* clothes.

At the corner of Second and Beale was a clothing store, run by the Lansky Brothers, that catered to black musicians. Elvis shopped there whenever he could afford to. If he had a little extra money, he would go to Lansky's and buy another pink shirt, or maybe a pink sportcoat with black lightning flashes on its lapels.

Elvis's hair and his taste in clothing contributed to the general impression that he was weird and different. "Had pretty long hair for that time, and I tell you it got pretty weird," Elvis said years later. "They used to see me coming down the street, and they'd say, 'Hot dang, let's get him, he's a squirrel, he's a squirrel, get him, he just come down outta the trees.' "[3]

Like nearly all the best rock-and-rollers, Elvis was misunderstood and not very popular at school. Almost no one outside his church knew that he sang, and he wasn't dating much. About the only notable thing that happened to him during his five years at Humes was that he was the surprise winner of the school talent show his senior year.

Red West was a year ahead of Elvis at Humes and played with him on the school's varsity football team, the Humes High Tigers. Elvis played just a year until the coach threw him off the team because he wouldn't cut his hair. As Red remembered, "Elvis had his hair real long in those days. He was the only guy. The rest of us had crew cuts. I remember once when all the guys were gonna get him and cut his hair I helped him escape from that. [Elvis] was just different. It gave the people something to do, to bother him."[4] Elvis didn't forget.

Even though he was hassled constantly by other teenagers who wanted him to act and dress as they did, Elvis insisted on doing things his own way, even if that meant being excluded. If that's how it was going to be, so be it. He always had his mother, and he always had the movies and the radio.

In the meantime, however, his family life slowly began to change. No longer walking her son to school, Gladys had gone to work as a nurse's aide at nearby St. Joseph's Hospital. As a direct result, the Presleys were evicted from the Lauderdale Courts because, taking Gladys's salary into account, the family's income exceeded the $3,000 maximum for public housing. For the first time in his life, Vernon was part of a family that was making too much money.

On January 7, 1953, the Presleys moved out of the Lauderdale Courts into a small apartment at 398 Cypress Street. That June, Elvis graduated from Humes High with an undistinguished mixture of B's and C's, and began looking for something to do with his life.

4

Sun 209

If only I could find a white boy who sang black, Sam Phillips used to say, I could make a million dollars. Then Phillips found Elvis.

Raised on his father's plantation, Sam Phillips grew up with the blues—the music, that is. As a child, he would sit at the feet of old black cotton pickers as they strummed out the blues late into the Alabama night. After college, Phillips moved to Memphis and became a radio announcer, coordinating broadcasts of orchestral music for $150 a week.

But Phillips didn't stay with that job very long. He was bored by the music, and he couldn't get the blues out of his head. So, despite having a wife and two young sons to support, he quit his radio job and instead opened a recording studio in 1951.

"It seemed to me that the Negroes were the only ones who had any freshness left in their music," Phillips recalled years later. But "there was no place in the South they could go to record. The nearest place where they made so-called 'race' records . . . was Chicago, and most of them didn't have the money or time to make the trip."[1]

Once Phillips opened his studio, though, the nearest place to record became Memphis, which was already quite close to the root of it all, the Mississippi Delta cotton country where the blues had been born and nurtured. At first, Phillips managed to pay his bills recording weddings and bar mitzvahs, but soon the blues began to pay off for him.

Phillips's original business involved recording local blues singers and then selling aluminum masters of these recordings to independent record companies such as Chess in Chicago and Modern Records in Los Angeles. (A master is a completed recording from which vinyl records are pressed.)

In the years between 1951, when Phillips first opened his studio, and 1953, when Elvis wandered in, Sam Phillips recorded the earliest efforts of singers who would later dominate the blues field. He recorded Howlin' Wolf and Bobby "Blue" Bland for Chess, and B. B. King and Big Walter Horton for Modern.

It was a living, but Phillips had even bigger plans. If the Chess brothers in Chicago and the Bihari brothers in Los Angeles could have their own indepedent record labels, so could Sam C. Phillips in Memphis. Encouraged by the success of his artists on other labels, Phillips founded Sun Records in 1952 so that he could release recordings himself.

In the early 1950s, the record business was dominated by a handful of national companies called the "majors." These companies included Columbia, RCA Victor, Decca, Capitol, MGM, and Mercury. Mostly, the majors recorded two kinds of music: Hit Parade pop and classical. They also recorded some country music. But Hit Parade pop was their specialty—songs like "I Saw Mommy Kissing Santa Claus" and "Till I Waltz Again with You." Because it was the only readily available popular music, Hit Parade pop dominated the charts. There just wasn't anything to compete with it.

And that's where the independent record companies saw their chance. The independent companies were smaller outfits than the majors and were able to operate on much smaller budgets because they didn't handle their own distribution. Instead of hiring and paying a sales force, "indie" labels hired independent distributors to get their records into the stores.

Because independent distributors took a cut of a record's sales rather than requiring cash up front, all you needed to start a record company was the money to press a few thousand singles. Using independent distributors meant low start-up costs and low overhead; it meant that you could produce regional hits and still make money. For music fans in the early fifties, it meant that a much wider range of music suddenly became available to them.

The teenage market was perfect for the new independent labels. And because the majors were unwilling to get involved in such rebellious, subcultural music as rhythm and blues, the field was left totally open to musical entrepreneurs such as Sam Phillips.

Almost immediately, Sun had a few regional hits with both Little Junior Parker and Rufus Thomas of WDIA. Parker did "Love My Baby" for Phillips and also wrote "Mystery Train," which Elvis later recorded as his last single for Sun.

Overconfident and stubborn, the majors refused to believe they were making a huge mistake. But the sales figures told a different story: Between 1946 and 1952, only five of the 162 million-selling records came from indies; by 1956, independents were responsible for just over half the Top Ten hits. Teenagers created the market, and then independents sprang up all over the country to meet the new demand.

In 1953, though, when Elvis left Humes, rock and roll was but a gleam in Sam Phillips's eye. Rhythm and blues was still the only antidote to the Hit Parade, and as popular as it was among hip teens, the market wasn't enormous. Most hits were regional, and independent labels had to hustle for whatever they could get.

Because Sun had its ups and downs, Phillips started the Memphis Recording Service to supplement his income. It was a make-your- own-record setup. For $4, you could cut two songs onto a 10-inch acetate single. As the story goes, Elvis walked in one day to record two songs.

By that time, the summer of 1953, Elvis had already been out of school for a few months. After his graduation from Humes, he had taken a factory job with the Precision Tool Company, but he quit almost immediately to take a job instead with the Crown Electric Company as a supply truck driver. Crown was conveniently located just a short walk from the Presleys' new place on Alabama Street, and the pay was $1.25 an hour, which worked out to about $41 a week after taxes.

Elvis seemed to be quite happy at Crown. He liked the working owners, James and Gladys Tipler, and the Tiplers liked Elvis, even though the length of his sideburns had thrown them at first. "Elvis used to like that hair," James Tipler remembered. "He used to wear it way back there! He'd come back from a run in the truck, and he'd go right to a mirror to comb his hair. Wouldn't be a time when he didn't do that, combing the hair just so."[2] (Elvis had his hair cut by a beautician, not a barber, which was very unusual for a truck driver in the summer of

1953.) Elvis even began studying at night to become an electrician, which he knew paid better than truck driving.

According to the legend, Elvis walked into the Memphis Recording Service at Sun's 706 Union Avenue studios to record a birthday present for his mother. But that story couldn't be right. Gladys's birthday was in April—and while no one could remember the exact date, all sources agree that Elvis first appeared at Sun sometime during the summer after the Humes graduation and while he was still working for Crown. It's not a crucial point, but it shows how Elvis's life story, and particularly his relationship with his mother, took on the qualities of myth.

When Elvis walked into the Memphis Recording Service to record the Ink Spots' "My Happiness" and "That's Where Your Heartaches Begin," he knew where

Elvis with Vernon and Gladys.

he was—a record company. And he also knew what he wanted to be—a singer. Sam Phillips discovered Elvis, but Elvis made it easy for him.

The Saturday afternoon that Elvis arrived, however, Phillips wasn't even there. Instead, his office manager, Marion Keisker, was running the studio. When Elvis's turn came to make a record, he stepped up to the microphone and launched right into "My Happiness," accompanying himself primitively on his own acoustic guitar. The singing was a bit wild and unformed, but something in Elvis's voice caught Keisker's ear. She thought it might be a good idea to tape this kid with the long sideburns for Phillips to hear when he came back. Fishing out a piece of discarded tape, she caught the second half of "My Happiness" and all of "That's When Your Heartaches Begin."

"Now this is something we never did, but I wanted Phillips to hear this, " Keisker said later. "I don't even know if Elvis knew I was taping it."[3]

When Phillips got back, Keisker played him the tape. Phillips said the boy needed a lot of work, but he was impressed. He made a note of Elvis's name and address, 462 Alabama Street, and even wrote down the phone number of a friend on the same block because the Presleys didn't have a phone. Elvis had told Keisker that this friend would come and fetch him if anyone ever called.

Six months later, on January 4, 1954—Phillips noted the date this time—Elvis showed up at Sun again to make another $4 acetate. He sang two more ballads, country ones this time. They were "Casual Love" and "I'll Never Stand in Your Way." Phillips told Elvis he liked what he heard, and that he'd call Elvis sometime.

Sometime turned out to be a couple of months later. A demo version of a song called "Without You" had come in from Nashville and Phillips liked it. In fact, he wanted to release the recording just as it was on the demo. Trouble was, he couldn't find out who the singer was. Just some black kid, he was told, who was hanging around the studio when the song came in. Without the singer's permission, however, Phillips couldn't release the record, so he was left with just one other option: find somebody else to record the song.

"How about the kid with the sideburns?" Keisker asked.[4] Grudgingly, Phillips agreed to let Keisker call Elvis. And that, as they say, was that.

"So I called and they went up the street and called Elvis to the phone," Keisker remembered. "I was still standing there with the telephone in my hand and here comes Elvis, panting. I think he ran all the way."[5]

Phillips played the "Without You" demo for Elvis, who then tried to sing it. The first take was terrible, and so was the second. Elvis kept trying but there was little improvement, so Phillips suggested that they take a break. It was obvious that if "Without You" was going to happen, it would have to happen without Elvis. But Phillips was interested in the kid anyway, and he asked Elvis what else he could do. "I can do anything," said Elvis. "Do it," said Phillips.[6] And Elvis was off, playing snatches of blues, gospel, country, Dean Martin pop— anything that came into his head that he thought might win Phillips over.

What was most obvious to Phillips, though, was that the kid needed work. The talent was there, but it needed form and polish. Elvis needed the help of a pro, so after the session Phillips called Scotty Moore. At that time, the spring of 1954, Moore was a 21-year-old guitarist with a western swing band called Doug Poindexter's Starlight Wranglers.

Elvis was wearing pink slacks, a pink shirt, and white buck shoes when he showed up at Scotty Moore's apartment that first time, a Sunday afternoon. There was a little awkwardness because Elvis was still shy around strangers, especially ones he thought were important. But once the guitars came out, everything settled down nicely. Elvis sang a few songs by Eddy Arnold and Hank Snow, two top country singers, and also a few by Billy Eckstine, the black rhythm-and-blues star.

About halfway through the two-hour session, Bill Black, the Starlight Wranglers' stand-up bass player, dropped by. He listened for a while and then left. No big deal, Black told Moore later. But Moore disagreed. He had heard something in Elvis's voice and kept working with him. Eventually, Moore convinced Black to change his mind and and join in, too.

"The talent was there, and it was extraordinary," rock and roll historian Greil Marcus wrote, "but it was complex, and it needed a form. They were in the studio a long, tiresome time to catch the spirit of a boy who, on record, sounded as if he flew in, stopped long enough to blow the walls back, and exited through the unhinged back door with a grin."[7]

A few months of hard work later, Scotty, Bill, and Elvis showed up at Sun for a rehearsal. Or it might have been a formal recording session—it all depends on the people you ask. But everyone agrees on the date: July 6, 1954. Write it down. Rock and roll was born that day.

There were four of them in that small studio. One workday was over, but another had just begun. In the cramped recording booth lined with acoustic tile, Scotty, Bill, and Elvis tuned up. Outside in the control booth, Sam Phillips worked the dials. There was only one microphone—because in those days before stereo, there was only one track.

Unlike the majors, who told their acts what songs to sing and how to sing them, the indies did business in a different way. Phillips's documentary recording style was typical. Basically, he turned on the machine and let the musicians feel their way around, much as they would in a bar or club.

The first song they played was "I Love You Because," and no one was happy with it. It sounded stiff, tight. Maybe Elvis was nervous. They tried a few other country songs and played back the tapes. Still nothing. Phillips suggested a break.

"Little while later," Scotty Moore said, "we were sitting there drinking a Coke, shooting the bull. So Elvis picked up his guitar and started banging on it and singing 'That's All Right Mama.' Just jumping around the studio, acting the fool."[8]

Elvis was just a kid then, 19, with a lot of energy to burn, and he was just letting some of it out. "That's All Right Mama" had been a minor hit for Big Boy Crudup a few years before, and Crudup had done it slow, in the traditional blues style. But Elvis was revving it up. No longer a tale of woe told by an old black man who'd seen plenty of trouble, "That's All Right" *moved* now.

Soon Black joined in, plucking out a matching rhythm on the bass. And then Moore chimed in with his electric guitar, picking out a high, jangly melody line. Nobody had ever heard anything like it before. It wasn't blues, and it wasn't country; it was something else.

All of a sudden, Phillips came running out of the control room because he'd just heard the sound of a million dollars—a white boy singing black. "What in the devil are you doing?" Phillips said. "We don't know," came the reply. "Well," Phillips answered back, "find out real quick and don't lose it."[9]

Most records date quickly. Musical styles change even faster than hairstyles, and records just a few years old already seem dead. But not "That's All Right Mama," which was Sun release No. 209. "That's All Right Mama" still sounds today as fresh and clean and free as it did the day it was laid down at 706 Union Avenue.

Like almost all traditional blues, the lyrics to "That's All Right Mama" are simple and repetitive. They are also vague, about nothing and everything, but it doesn't matter. What does matter is Elvis and what he does with them on the record. He jumps with them and dances with them. He skips them across a shining bright lake and then jumps into the cool water after them. He makes them soar, and he makes them strut.

When Phillips played the tape back, Moore and Black agreed that the track was exciting. "But, good God," one of the group said, "they'll run us outta town when they hear it."[10]

The first thing Phillips did with "That's All Right Mama," even before pressing the record, was take a copy of the master to Dewey Phillips (no relation), host of the popular "Red Hot And Blue" show on Memphis's WHBQ. WHBQ was a white radio station, but the "Red

Hot And Blue" show was devoted exclusively to the blues, and that meant music by blacks. It was WHBQ's way of luring back all those white teenagers who had abandoned the station for WDIA and KWEM.

Because Dewey liked "That's All Right," he put the record on the air right away. Immediately, the switchboard lit up. Knowing how to ride a good thing, Dewey played the track again. And again. In all, he played the record more than thirty times that night. In fact, things got so out of hand that Dewey called Elvis to ask him to come down to the station. Elvis was at the Suzore No. 2, of course, and Vernon and Gladys had to wander the aisles until they found him.

"I don't know nothing about being interviewed," Elvis confessed at the station. "Just don't say nothing dirty, son," Dewey replied.[11] Then Dewey had Elvis talk about going to Humes, which was all-white at the time. "I wanted to get that out," Dewey said later, "because a lot of people listening had thought he was colored."[12]

"That's All Right Mama" was such an overnight success that less than a week after Dewey played the record, Phillips had already received back orders for six thousand copies.

After the record broke, Elvis began playing ballrooms around town as a guest artist with the Starlight Wranglers, and then just with Scotty and Bill. At first, the promoters called Elvis the "Hillbilly Cat." Then they called him the "King of Western Bop." But even though a lot of people went to a lot of trouble to find a name for this new music, nothing stuck.

Eventually, the early form of rock and roll developed at Sun did get a name: rockabilly. As names go, it was a simple one. The beat rocked like rhythm and blues, while the guitar danced around and jangled just as it did in "hillbilly" music. Rockabilly was the music that proved white boys could be just as extreme, just as daring and free, as blacks.

The Memphis blues style favored small bands and simple arrangments—usually not much more than piano, saxophone, guitar, and vocals. But rockabilly was even simpler, with no horns at all and not much piano either. It was just guitars, guitars, and more guitars: Elvis's acoustic rhythm, Scotty Moore's electric lead, and Bill Black's bass.

From there to pure rock and roll, the transition was simple—just add drums. In a rock and roll band, the definitive line-up is a lead guitar, a rhythm guitar, a bass guitar, and drums. The bass and drums set the beat at the bottom of the sound, the lead guitarist picks out the melody at the top, and the strums of the rhythm guitarist fill in the middle. What made rock and roll different from the blues was that its beat was young and hopeful rather than bluesy and subdued. Why deal with unpleasant reality before you have to? the beat was saying. You're young, went the rhythm. Show it.

The beat was very important. It was the most immediately obvious thing about rock and roll. It was bigger and faster than any beat before it. It was aggressive and sexual and noisy. But you really had to mean it to make it work. Elvis had grown up poor and been as outside as any black. Elvis *meant* it.

The change from Memphis blues to rock and roll wasn't limited to instruments and sound, however. It was the whole idea of the music that changed. Unlike the slow and mournful blues, white teenage rock and roll was fast and wild and open to possibilities.

And then there was Elvis, urging everyone on. "Milkcow Blues Boogie," Elvis's third release on Sun in January 1955, begins as a loping blues number. Then Elvis stops the song. "Hold it, fellas," he says. "That don't move me! Let's get real, real gone for a change." And before you realize what's going on, "Milkcow Blues" comes at you twice as hard and twice as fast.

Much of Elvis's immediate, shocking impact can be traced to the fact that his audience was already familiar with the songs he was singing. People knew Big Boy Crudup's version of "That's All Right Mama," and they knew the original recording of "Milk Cow Blues" made by Kokomo Arnold, its author, in Chicago in 1934. But to hear Elvis do these songs was a revelation. There had never been music like this before.

Not that others weren't also trying to push back the limits of popular music. In the early fifties, the music world was starved for something new. A veteran of the western swing circuit, Bill Haley, had been thinking about the situation for a few years already. "The days of the solo vocalist and the big bands had gone," Haley remembered. "I felt then that if I could take, say, a Dixie- land [jazz] tune and drop the first and third beats, and accentuate the second and fourth, and add a beat the listeners could clap [and dance to], this would be what they were after."[13]

The result was something special: Bill Haley and His Comets' "Rock Around the Clock," which hit Number One on the pop charts on July 9, 1955, and stayed there for eight weeks.

Haley, though, was no Elvis. The reason rock and roll is more closely associated with Elvis's recordings for Sun is that Bill Haley was not a teenager, either in age or temperament. Already in his late twenties, Haley was hardly dangerous. He was married with five kids, moon-faced, a little chubby, and obviously no threat at all, sexually or otherwise. Instead, he was a clever professional musician who had recognized a hole in the musical culture and then filled it. He consciously mixed styles and kept trying different combinations until one finally hit.

Elvis, though, embodied the tensions that made rock and roll so dynamic. He was both city and country, black and white, rebellious and respectful all at the same time. He was the ultimate teenager, and for that reason he would also become the ultimate teen idol.

Elvis was as suprised as anyone at what he had created. "I don't know what it is," he confessed to the *Saturday Evening Post* in 1956. "I just fell into it, really. My daddy and I were laughing about it the other day. He looked at me and said, 'What happened, El? The last thing I can remember is I was working in a can factory, and you were driving a truck.' We all feel the same way about it still. It just . . . caught us up."[14]

5

Have You Heard the News?

With all that has happened in the years since Elvis first made those ground-breaking records for Sun, it's sometimes easy to wonder what all the fuss was about. But try to imagine yourself as a teenager in 1954. Dwight Eisenhower, the president, seemed to spend most of his time playing golf. The Number One song in the country was a syrupy ballad, "Three Coins in the Fountain." The revolutionary new household appliance was the color television. Mothers were dressing their children in bow ties and sensible shoes. Then Elvis came along and . . . WOW! Everybody got real, real gone for a change.

Country singer Bob Luman once described what attending an early Elvis show was like for a fifties teenager aching for something new and different:

> This cat came out in red pants and a green coat and a pink shirt and socks, and he had this sneer on his face and he stood behind the mike for five minutes, I'll bet, before he made a move. Then he hit his guitar a lick, and he broke two strings. I'd been playing ten years, and I hadn't broken a total of two strings. So there he was, these two strings dangling, and he hadn't done anything yet, and these high school girls were screaming and fainting and running up to the stage, and then he started to move his hips real slow like he

had a thing for his guitar. That was Elvis Presley when he was about 19, playing Kilgore, Texas. He made chills run up my back, man, like when your hair starts grabbing at your collar.[1]

Elvis's early success was fragile, however, and as long as he was at Sun, each new record risked it. There was always the danger of disappointment: the more you expect, the harder it becomes to accept failure. But whatever the risks, Elvis wasn't turning back—it was all or nothing, and you could hear it in his voice.

At first, there was a lot of resistance from disk jockeys. One reason was that the new music didn't fit the deejays' preconceived notions of what popular music should be. It was so different that nobody knew just what to make of it. Another reason was that, while segregation was still in effect, it was difficult to promote "integrated" music in the South—that is, a white boy who sang black.

In Memphis, though, there was a lot of black music already on the radio, so it wasn't too hard for Elvis to get airplay. And once people heard this new sensation, everybody just had to buy his records. Based on his success in Memphis with "That's All Right Mama," Elvis got what, at the time, seemed to be the most important break of his career—a fall booking to perform at the Grand Ole Opry in Nashville.

Started in 1925, the Grand Ole Opry was, for years, a cornerstone of the American popular music establishment. It was the Carnegie Hall of country music. In the days before television, families all over the country would gather around the radio to listen to the Opry's famous Saturday night broadcasts. "For all of us,"

Marion Keisker said, "the Grand Ole Opry was the summit, the peak, the show you hoped you'd get eventually— not when you had just one record out."[2]

From the beginning, however, the Opry's talent coordinator, Jim Denny, wasn't happy. When he saw only Elvis, Scotty, and Bill, he asked where the rest of the musicians were. He said he had paid for the band that had played on the record, and that's what he wanted. He couldn't believe that only three guys had made that much sound.

And later, after the show, Denny still wasn't happy. When it was over, he went up to Elvis and told him to consider going back to driving a truck. Elvis was crushed; according to another Opry performer, he cried all the way home.

Elvis was just too unusual for the traditionalist Opry. But the last thing Phillips wanted to do was tone Elvis down. Instead, he played up Elvis's difference as much as possible. On each of the five Sun records that Elvis made between July 1954 and November 1955, for example, Phillips made sure to pair a country song with a blues number. If there ever could be a formula for Elvis, Phillips was sure it would include blues and country in equal parts.

Encouraged by Phillips, Elvis didn't give up, either. Instead he followed up his Opry date with an October 1954 booking on the "Lousiana Hayride" radio show out of Shreveport, Louisiana. His spot on the "Hayride" was much more successful. In fact, the producers liked Elvis so much they brought him back again and then offered him a year-long contract to appear once a week. Elvis agreed.

Elvis at the Louisiana Hayride.

Through the "Hayride," Elvis became friendly with the show's staff drummer, D. J. Fontana, who soon joined Elvis's band. "He was pretty hot," Fontana remembered of Elvis's first night on the "Hayride." "He tore the house down. He was the kingpin. Horace Logan was program director for the station and when Horace heard Elvis that first time, he did fourteen back flips."[3]

With the "Hayride" contract under his belt, Elvis soon began to make money—enough, at any rate, so that he could afford to quit his job at Crown. According to his boss there, James Tipler, "[Elvis came] to us finally and he said he didn't think he could keep on working nights, playing his music and singing, and still give us a good day's work, too, so he left."[4]

Around this time, the winter of 1954-55, Colonel Tom Parker began to get interested in Elvis. Parker had a very colorful past. To begin with, his rank of colonel, as everyone well knew, was utterly self-appointed. Colonel Tom's career had been entirely in show business. It began with a job as a carnival barker, which exploited his greatest talent: his ability to tread the line between salesman and con man—and not get arrested.

As Parker told the story, he was born in 1910 in West Virginia, where his parents were touring with a circus. Also according to Parker, his parents died before he was 10, and he ended up with his uncle's traveling show, the Great Parker Pony Circus. Legend has it that at one time Colonel Tom made a living painting sparrows yellow and selling them as canaries.

Parker was a lot like P. T. Barnum, the famous circus entrepreneur who once said, "There's a sucker born every minute." Colonel Tom said, "Don't explain it, just sell it." After a while, though, Parker decided he had had enough of the midway, and he switched over to carnival promotion, working as a press agent for a series of circuses and showboats. Finally, he settled down during the 1930s with his wife and son in Tampa, Florida.

At first, Colonel Tom had a regular job doing promotional work for the Tampa humane society, but he soon began taking on more and more freelance promotional assignments. That's how he became involved in music: promoting, on a freelance basis, the country music shows that passed through Tampa. Through these shows, Colonel Tom met Eddy Arnold and Hank Snow, both major country stars whose careers he would later manage on and off.

Through the influence of Arnold and primarily Snow, Tom Parker became, by 1955, a very important man in the country music business. As head of Hank Snow Jamboree Attractions, one of the largest booking agencies in the South, Colonel Tom made deals and got around. Oscar Davis, a Parker advance man, happened to hear Elvis's record during a trip to Memphis that winter, and he tipped the Colonel off.

Parker didn't act very impressed at first, but when *Billboard* named Elvis the eighth most promising newcomer in its annual survey—on the basis of just one record—Colonel Tom began to sniff around Elvis like a bloodhound on the scent.

Elvis had never really had a full-time manager. At first, Scotty Moore had taken an extra cut of their earnings in exchange for arranging the bookings. Then a Memphis disk jockey, Bob Neal, took over. But even Neal realized that Elvis would soon be much too big for a deejay to handle. In February 1955, Elvis accepted Colonel Tom's offers of help.

Right away, Parker began booking Elvis with the Hank Snow Jamboree as it toured the South and Southwest. Elvis played in New Mexico, Texas, Lousiana, Alabama, Florida, and Virginia. Meanwhile, working through Vernon and Gladys, Colonel Tom slowly began to exert control. Promising lots of money and even greater success, Parker soon convinced the Presleys that only he knew what was best for their boy. Although the Colonel didn't officially sign Elvis to a management contract until the spring of 1956, it was during 1955 that he personally took over Elvis's career.

The most important move Parker made for Elvis was to engineer RCA Victor's buyout of his Sun recording contract. As a regional independent, Sun was limited, and Colonel Tom knew that for Elvis to really cash in he'd have to go with a major. Ahmet Ertegun of Atlantic Records, the largest of the indies, was willing to hock everything to pay $25,000 for Elvis, an unprecedented sum at the time. But Parker held out for a major.

Colonel Tom knew the people at RCA Victor because both Eddy Arnold and Hank Snow had recorded for the label. When he contacted RCA, however, he found out that the big bosses weren't interested at all in Elvis or in rock and roll. They were sure the fad would pass, and they didn't want to be bothered with it.

But Steve Sholes, RCA's talent scout in Nashville, didn't share that opinion. On the contrary, Sholes insisted that the company buy Elvis's contract. And because his track record at RCA had been so exceptional, the label decided to take the risk.

It didn't take very long for the arrangements to be made. Then, in November 1955, at the annual disk jockeys' convention in Nashville, it was announced publicly that Elvis had been sold to RCA. The price: $35,000 to Sun plus a $5,000 bonus to Elvis, who used the money to buy his mother a new pink Cadillac. Pink was Elvis's favorite color, and the Cadillac name proved that he was a poor boy no longer. For many people, this particular car came to symbolize Elvis, his flashiness and his money. And later, it also came to symbolize America itself at that time. Plush and opulent, the 1955 Cadillac convertible was built not only for transportation but also for speed and showing off.

In the years that followed the sale of Elvis's contract, Sam Phillips was routinely second-guessed by almost everyone. If only he hadn't sold Elvis! people sighed.

Elvis with Colonel Tom.

What a mistake! But when Phillips let Elvis go, it didn't seem like a mistake at all. Maybe Elvis would have made the big time on Sun, or maybe he wouldn't have. In any event, he would have had much less of a chance than he did at RCA, where there was much more money available to promote him. Also, $35,000 was a lot of cash in 1955, enough to turn Sun from a struggling regional outfit into an independent strong enough to perhaps break a record or two. Besides, Phillips felt that having found an Elvis once, he could simply do it again.

Of course, it later turned out that Elvis was much more unusual than Phillips or anyone else (with the exception of Gladys) had believed possible. But Phillips did use RCA's money to produce some very good and very profitable records. Once Elvis broke through the pop barrier, other poor white southerners rose out of the cotton fields and beat a path to Phillips's door. Among them were Johnny Cash, Jerry Lee Lewis, Carl Perkins, and Roy Orbison. Sun lost Elvis, but with RCA's money Sam Phillips didn't do too badly. Not at all.

Elvis spent Christmas that year back in Memphis with his parents before traveling to Nashville on January 5, 1956, for his first RCA recording session with Steve Sholes. At Sun, it had been just Elvis and Scotty Moore on guitar, Bill Black on bass, and sometimes D. J. Fontana on drums. But Sholes had other ideas. He added some studio musicians, including guitarist Chet Atkins, and a vocal group, the Jordanaires, to fill out the sound.

Elvis's Sun recordings had been lean and hard in the rockabilly style, but that wasn't the sound RCA was after. In order to promote Elvis simultaneously in all three major markets—pop, country, and rhythm and blues—

Sholes was looking to ease the sharpest edges and make Elvis sound bigger and softer at the same time. To accomplish this, he had the Jordanaires back up Elvis on a few ballads and added a piano here and there for richness.

Extreme and raw, Sun rockabilly had displayed Elvis's rebel side. But there was more to Elvis Aron Presley than his loud pink shirts and his sneer. For all his arrogance and sexuality, Elvis was still Gladys's devoted son. His music may have infuriated other people's parents; but against *his* parents, Elvis wasn't rebelling at all. Mostly what he wanted was to be a star. In his mind, he didn't owe rockabilly anything. There was no principle involved, such as being "true" to the music. Far from it. Having been on the outside all his life, Elvis simply wanted success and the money and fame that came along with it. He wanted to cash in. Colonel Tom helped, of course.

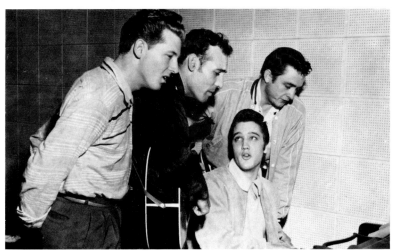

Sun's million-dollar quartet: Jerry Lee Lewis, Carl Perkins, Johnny Cash, and Elvis Presley.

6

Hail, Hail, Rock and Roll

From the start, Tom Parker was an unlikely revolution maker. It just didn't make sense that a jaded show business professional like Parker could help launch a music as rebellious as rock and roll. But that was rock's commercial paradox: First and foremost, people were in it for the money. It didn't matter whether the Colonel liked Elvis's music or not; all that mattered, to Parker and to RCA alike, was whether teenagers bought Presley's records.

"When I found Elvis, the boy had nothing but a million dollars' worth of talent," the Colonel was fond of saying. "Now he has a million dollars."[1] Actually, this was an understatement. From 1956 on, Elvis never earned less than $1 million a year. In most years, he earned quite a bit more.

Elvis's success came so suddenly and with such intensity that it still seems a bit mystifying. The concerts and the recording sessions all blurred together. Most days Elvis couldn't tell you where he had been or where he was going. But Colonel Tom knew. No one can say what would have happened to Elvis had he stayed at Sun, whether he would have made it or not. In the music business, as in any other, talent alone is not enough to guarantee success. But there's no doubt that Elvis would not have become the phenomenon he did if it hadn't been for the Colonel.

Elvis's first record for RCA, "Heartbreak Hotel," recorded during the January 1956 Nashville sessions, became the Number One song in the country on April 21. It was the first of what RCA claimed were fourteen consecutive million-sellers for the King. Making the charts for the first time the week of March 10, "Heartbreak Hotel" stuck around for twenty-two weeks, including eight at Number One. The follow-ups—"Hound Dog," "Don't Be Cruel," and "Love Me Tender"—gave Elvis the Number One spot from August of 1956 all the way through until December.

Soon the money came pouring in, and record royalties were only part of it. Elvis was a multimedia sensation; his name alone could sell a product. Almost overnight, it was in all the department stores, emblazoned across no fewer than seventy-five different kinds of merchandise from Elvis Presley pajamas to Elvis Presley soda to the Elvis Presley game. By the end of 1957, one retailer estimated merchandising sales at $55 million.

In this way, Elvis, more than anyone else, solidified rock and roll's commercial potential. As rock critic Nik Cohn pointed out, "Before Elvis, rock had been a gesture of vague rebellion. Once he'd happened, it immediately became solid, self-contained; and then it spawned its own style in clothes and language."[2] Elvis represented something much more than just a pop music star: he was the symbol of a youth that spoke its own language, had its own heroes, and cared little for the standards of its parents' generation. Needless to say, many parents weren't too happy about that last part.

But what could they do about it? Already, the Elvis revolution was just too big for them. In just one year, four hundred thousand teenagers had joined the Elvis Presley Fan Club. In his first six months at RCA, Elvis sold eight million records. By 1957, Elvis was himself, personally, a $20-million-a-year industry. You could buy an awful lot of pink Cadillacs with that kind of money.

His first national television appearance was on the Tommy and Jimmy Dorsey "Stage Show" on January 28, 1956. For six Saturday nights, Elvis was paid $1,250 per show. Later, on April 3, Elvis appeared on "The Milton Berle Show" before an audience estimated at forty million people, or one in every four Americans.

The next stop for Elvis was Steve Allen's new Sunday night variety show on NBC. Allen was in close competition with "Toast of the Town," Ed Sullivan's Sunday night variety show on CBS. For Elvis's July appearance, Steve Allen pulled more than 55 percent of the viewing audience, while Sullivan was left with 15 percent. The same week, Sullivan began negotiations with the Colonel.

Steve Allen had paid Elvis $7,500 for a single appearance; Sullivan offered $50,000 for three shows. Averaged out over the three shows, Sullivan's offer more than tripled his show's previous highwater mark of $5,000 per appearance.

September 9, 1956, the date Elvis appeared on Sullivan's show, was the climax of his rocketlike rise. Among young and old alike there was great anticipation. "Toast of the Town" was famous for its spectacle. So was Elvis. Few dared predict what might happen.

Elvis sang only two songs that night in September, but Sullivan still got his money's worth: an 82.6 percent share of the viewing audience, equal to about fifty-four million people. That kind of number was unheard of. President Eisenhower's speech accepting the 1956 Republican presidential nomination carried on all three networks had attracted only fifty-one million viewers. It was a record, and the record stood until 1964, when the Beatles' debut on Ed Sullivan broke it.

Elvis's appearance on Ed Sullivan is also famous for a reason that has nothing to do with television ratings or record sales. It has to do with the fear of rock and roll, which Sullivan had in large measure. Earlier, Sullivan had vowed that he would never hire a rock and roller like Presley under any circumstances. He had called Elvis "unfit for a family audience."[3] After Steve Allen's ratings later forced him to put Elvis on the show, Sullivan still gave orders to the cameramen to show Elvis only from the waist up. There'd be no swiveling hips on Ed Sullivan's show.

Unfortunately for Elvis and his fans, Sullivan wasn't the only grown-up getting all hot and bothered about rock and roll. As far as these self-appointed defenders of the community's morals were concerned, Elvis in particular and rock and roll music in general were an affront to everything that was decent and good in America.

In the *New York Times,* music critic Jack Gould crusaded against Elvis. "Mr. Presley has no discernible singing ability," Gould wrote in the formal *Times* style. "His one specialty is an accentuated movement of the body that heretofore has been primarily identified with the repertoire of the blonde bombshells of the burlesque runway."[4]

"It isn't enough to say that Elvis is kind to his parents," wrote another critic. "That still isn't a free ticket to behave like a sex maniac in public before millions of impressionable kids."[5]

The backlash against rock and roll came from inside the record business, too—notably from those majors such as Columbia who were losing their market shares to rock and roll indies such as Sun and Chess. Mitch Miller, the man at Columbia who decided which acts the company would sign and what songs they would sing, became famous for his pronouncement that rock and roll couldn't possibly last. (Miller, incidentally, had called Sam Phillips about Elvis's contract just one year before, but hung up when he heard Phillips's asking price.) Frank Sinatra, himself once a much bewailed teen idol, told a congressional committee that rock and roll was "the most brutal, ugly, desperate, vicious form of expression it has been my misfortune to hear."[6]

San Antonio, Texas, banned rock and roll from being played at the city's public swimming pools. In Ottawa, Canada, eight students from the Notre Dame Convent school were expelled for attending an Elvis concert. In Asbury Park, New Jersey, all rock and roll concerts were banned after twenty-five "vibrating teenagers" were hospitalized following a record hop. Under public pressure, radio stations all around the country burned, broke, or sold off their Presley records. In fact, there was such an outcry against the music that it made teenagers think there might be a conspiracy to put a lid on rock and roll.

What kind of music provoked this reaction? There was Elvis, of course. But he had a little help.

Once Elvis showed them how it was done, they all came cruising out of the swamps and the cotton fields—white boys who wanted to sing black. Many ended up at

Sun. One of these was Jerry Lee Lewis from northern Louisiana.

Jerry Lee was a lot like Elvis, only more so. Elvis acted dangerous, but Jerry Lee really was dangerous. He called himself "the Killer," and nobody was quite sure whether the nickname was literal or not.

Jerry Lee was wild, and so was his music. His first big hit for Sun, "Whole Lotta Shakin' Goin' On," was so uptempo that it was hard even for Lewis's backup band to keep up as the singer's fingers flew across his piano's keyboard. If ever a record sounded like a Saturday night bar fight, this was it.

Jerry Lee's performance style was totally hyperactive. He jumped around and bounced off the walls, all the time banging on the piano and sometimes even playing it with his feet. One time, an interviewer asked Jerry Lee the names of the musicians who played on his records. "I played on 'em," the Killer said. "What else do you need to know?"[7]

Another Sun performer was Carl Perkins. Like Bill Haley, Perkins was a professional musician who consciously mixed styles in order to cook up a fresh sound that might be commercially successful. Also like Haley, Perkins made one spectacular contribution. It was "Blue Suede Shoes," a song about a pair of loud, blue suede shoes and how nobody should step on them because they're so new and hip and cool. Perkins had a pretty good run with that song, but then Elvis recorded it for his first RCA album. When Elvis sang it, you could really believe the idea that clothes were important to your life.

In the meantime, most blacks still played rhythm and blues. There wasn't much difference left between rock and roll and R & B. But there was still segregation. Rock and roll had been born out of black music, but you didn't find many blacks playing it because you just didn't hear blacks on white radio stations. Not at first, anyway. But as rock and roll began to take over the charts, smart, young R & B men like Chuck Berry, realizing that the white market was where the real money was, began to write and play songs that might have crossover appeal.

Chuck Berry

Always a hustler, Berry had worked on a Ford assembly line and as a hairdresser before he started playing rhythm and blues professionally. In fact, when Berry first left for Chicago in 1955 to peddle a homemade demo tape, he was still hoping to make it in R & B. He went to see Leonard Chess, who was the head of Chess Records, then the premier label in urban rhythm and blues.

The two cuts Berry played for Chess were "Wee Wee Hours," a blues number that Chuck thought was his best shot at a hit, and a more offbeat song called "Ida Red," an adapted country tune. Leonard Chess liked "Wee Wee Hours," but he knew it was "Ida Red" that sounded like a hit. After renaming the tune "Maybellene," Chess brought it to Alan Freed in New York, then rock and roll's top disk jockey. Freed spun "Maybellene" all the way up to Number Five.

"I liked it," Leonard Chess recalled about "Ida Red," "thought it was something new. I was going to New York anyway, and I took a dub [copy] to Alan and said, 'Play this.' The dub didn't have Chuck's name on it or nothing. By the time I got back to Chicago, Freed had called a dozen times, saying it was his biggest record ever. History, the rest, y'know?"

"Sure," Chess went on, "'Wee Wee Hours' . . . was a good tune too, but the kids wanted the big beat, cars, and young love. It was a trend and we jumped on it."[8]

"Maybellene" is a rock and roll classic. It's all there: the driving beat, the rumbling bass, the throaty rhythm guitar, the flashy lead. And over it all, Chuck Berry rolls out those epic lyrics about a guy and a girl and a car. Someone once asked Berry why he wrote so many songs about cars. "It's because everybody has one," he said.[9]

Chuck Berry's sound was distinctively urban because it was so electric and so guitar-intensive, much like the Chicago style of R & B. But unlike the Chicago bluesmen, Chuck Berry deliberately went after the white market. In songs such as "School Days," "Sweet Little Sixteen," and "Almost Grown," he consistently wrote about the day-to-day travails of teenage life. Chuck Berry's style was clever and fast, but he was never really out of control. That was for Little Richard, who was wild—as wild as Jerry Lee, maybe even wilder, and explicitly sexual. Little Richard understood, perhaps as no one else, that rock and roll had to be as loud, as rude, and as physically demanding as possible. Otherwise, parents might like it.

Born in Macon, Georgia, on Christmas Day, 1935, Richard Penniman came from a family of preachers, though his father was a bootlegger. At the age of 13, he was kicked out of his house because his father was no longer willing to tolerate the boy's bizarre behavior, his peculiar taste in clothing—and, most of all, his noise.

"I came from a family," Richard once explained, "where my people didn't like rhythm and blues. Bing Crosby, 'Pennies from Heaven,' Ella Fitzgerald, was all I heard. And I knew that there was something that could be louder than that, but I didn't know where to find it. And I found it was me."[10]

Little Richard's sound was nothing if not loud. Like Elvis and most of the other early southern rockers, Richard learned how to sing in church. But Richard was a Baptist, and Baptists wail. When Little Richard entered adolescence and found rhythm and blues, he stopped singing for the Lord, but he didn't stop wailing.

Yet there was more to Richard's style than his un-matched decibel level. Equally important to his sound were the sharp and dynamic shifts in pitch that punc-tuated his songs like bursts of anti-aircraft fire, and the vocal gymnastics that Richard would perform with whatever syllables came easiest to the tongue. While Elvis sometimes crooned, Richard always attacked, and usually with only the barest modicum of taste. There was no way fifties parents could like Little Richard.

Little Richard

The story of Little Richard's first session for Specialty Records, another indie, sounds much like the story of Elvis's first Sun session. The tunes that Richard had - prepared all turned out to be incredibly dull. But during a break Richard began loosening up with a crude little ditty he had made up a few months earlier. He called it "Tutti Frutti," just because the phrase was easy to shout over and over again.

On the record of "Tutti Frutti" he cut that day, Little Richard sounds nearly hysterical. He plays his voice the way Jerry Lee Lewis played his piano, jumping on top of the thing and pounding every last ounce of energy and volume out of it. At times, Richard's producer, Bumps Blackwell, had to put some cardboard between Richard's mouth and the microphone because he was just too loud.

Later, when "Tutti Frutti" was released, many music critics used it as an example of how pointless and silly rock and roll lyrics were. But all the critics proved was that they just didn't get it. To his teenage audience, Richard's lyrics made a lot of sense. It was all in the way he sang them.

"I was washing dishes at the Greyhound bus station at the time," Richard said of his inspiration for "Tutti Frutti." "I couldn't talk back to my boss man. He would bring all these pots back to me to wash, and one day I said, 'A-wop-bop-a-lu-bop a-wop-bam-boom, take 'em out!' And that's what I meant at the time."[11]

Taken altogether, this kind of music bedeviled the major record companies, mostly because they couldn't control it and didn't own it. Between 1955 and 1958, the majors' share of singles action on the pop charts halved. Something had to be done.

A few majors tried signing rock and roll acts, but since no one at these companies liked the music, it was nearly impossible for them to tell which were the best bands. Instead, the preferred strategy was the "cover," a song originally performed by one singer that is then recorded by another. Elvis's "Blue Suede Shoes," for example, was a cover of Carl Perkins's original.

During the fifties, however, when the majors did covers of rock and roll songs, they used clean-cut white acts with names like the Crewcuts and the Four Preps to bleach the music. They usually changed the lyrics as well, just in case. Some of the best-known covers were made by bland and blue-eyed Pat Boone, who had a string of hits for Dot covering songs by black performers like Fats Domino and even Little Richard. Boone had at least five inches less hair than Richard, at *least*, but his pasteurized cover of "Tutti Frutti" had a ten-week chart run, peaking at Number Twelve. Richard's original, with much less promotional muscle behind it, charted for just five weeks and made it only to Number Seventeen. Clearly, there was a market for covers—but to those not dazzled by the promotion, it did indeed seem as though there was a conspiracy against the music.

In the meantime, Elvis made even more money. He toured all over the country, and even returned to Tupelo to play the Mississippi-Alabama Farm and Dairy Show. The city rolled out the red carpet, declaring September 28, 1956, to be Elvis Presley Day and presenting the King with a three-foot-long guitar-shaped key to the city.

Elvis's fee for the show was $5,000 or 60 percent of the ticket sales, whichever was more (a special low price for Tupelo). The hometown boy made $10,000 that day. But on his way out of town, he signed the check back over to the city. No doubt Colonel Tom had some pretty mixed feelings: the resulting publicity was good, but so was the money.

"I consider it my patriotic duty to keep Elvis up in the 90 percent tax bracket," Colonel Tom declared.[12] RCA had done its part; now it was 20th Century Fox's turn.

Sitting all those nights in the Suzore No. 2, Elvis had dreamed of being a movie star. Finally, that dream was coming true. A Hollywood producer had seen Elvis on the Dorsey Brothers television show and had arranged for a screen test. When that went well, Elvis was offered a contract.

Fox officials asked Colonel Tom whether $25,000 would be an adequate fee for the first film, *Love Me Tender*, considering that Elvis had never acted before. The Colonel's response was pleasant enough. "That's fine for me," he said. "Now, what about the boy?"[13] The figure Fox and Parker finally settled on was $1 million for each of Elvis's first four films.

The first film, originally titled *The Reno Brothers* but renamed *Love Me Tender* to cash in on Elvis's latest hit, was one of his better acting efforts. Released in November 1956, it tells the Civil War story of two brothers in love with the same girl. Elvis's character dies at the end. It's very tragic. But the critics were nearly unanimous: they didn't like it. Still, Elvis's fans did, and the film grossed more than five times what it cost to make.

A year later, Elvis's third film, *Jailhouse Rock*, got even worse reviews, but by then Elvis had gotten used to them. One critic said that Elvis had been "sensitively cast as a slob." Elvis said, "That's the way the mop flops."[14]

7

GI Blues

So there was Elvis. He couldn't be much happier. He was a rock and roll star. He was a movie star. Already he owned three Cadillacs, a three-wheeled Messerschmitt, and a new home, Graceland, in Memphis.

Elvis bought Graceland in March 1957, after it had fallen into disrepair. For the next three months, construction crews worked seven days a week and most nights, too, readying the thirteen-room mansion for the Presleys. Elvis intended Graceland to be a palace for Gladys, and soon she was surrounded by maids, who washed and ironed her clothing as soon as she took it off, and cooks, who would prepare meals around the clock if necessary. No luxury was too frivolous for Elvis. Whether or not he knew that money couldn't buy everything, he certainly wanted everything money could buy.

Once Graceland was set up, Elvis went back to Hollywood to make *Jailhouse Rock*. After that, he toured the Northwest and then took a few weeks off to vacation at the Sea and Sand Hotel in Biloxi, Mississippi. Elvis was back at Graceland for Christmas, though, when it came: his draft notice. The date was December 20, 1957. Uncle Sam wanted him for the army.

The draft notice was inevitable. In the 1950s, the draft was very much a reality, and Elvis's number was bound to come up sooner or later. It's just that December 1957 was a lot sooner than anyone had expected.

Throughout the music business, the question on everyone's mind was: What would happen to rock and roll now? The majors—with the exception of Elvis's label, RCA Victor—were delighted. Rock and roll had been hurting their sales badly, and anything that slowed the rock juggernaut would have to be good for their business.

From the teenage point of view, of course, the drafting of Elvis made perfect sense: It proved once more the existence of an adult conspiracy against their music.

Elvis and the Colonel were pretty happy, though. For Elvis, induction meant, finally, a relief from the constant strain of being Elvis the Pelvis, King of Rock and Roll. In the army, he could be just one of the guys, Private E. Presley, Serial Number 53310761. And to the Colonel's mind, the army was just what Elvis's image needed. As long as Elvis worked up a backlog of product, the two-year hitch could be a very good thing, transforming Elvis from a gyrating teenage dynamo to an all-American, flag-waving boy.

At the request of Paramount, Elvis applied for a sixty-day deferment so that he could finish his fourth film, *King Creole*. But it was the last request Elvis would make of the army. From here on in, the Colonel told the press, Elvis would be just one more boy doing his duty and serving his country.

On March 24, 1958, at 6:30 in the morning, Elvis appeared at the Memphis draft board for his induction. Vernon and Gladys were with him, as well as a few of the Memphis Mafia, Elvis's gang of friends and bodyguards. Colonel Tom was also there, handing out balloons that advertised *King Creole* to crowds of teenage girls who had gathered outside. Dozens of reporters and pho-

Elvis in the army.

tographers captured everything from Elvis's blood tests to his loyalty oath. Later, Elvis was shipped out to Fort Chaffee, Arkansas, where three hundred girls were already waiting at the gate for him. The Colonel, of course, had made arrangements for the press to follow.

Elvis began his first full day in the army at 5:30 A.M., March 25. At breakfast, a horde of photographers captured every mouthful of sausage and every swallow of coffee. Including Elvis, there were fifty recruits in the mess hall; there were fifty-five members of the press.

The main event of the day, however, came after lunch: the haircut that would make history of Elvis's famous sideburns and ducktail. Army barber James Peterson of Gans, Oklahoma, did the honors. He wrapped a towel around Elvis's shoulders, switched on his electric clippers, and—pausing momentarily while the photographers' flashbulbs exploded around him—proceeded to give Elvis his first crew cut. "Hair today, gone tomorrow," Elvis said.[1]

At first, it had been assumed by most people that Elvis would go into Special Services, which is the branch of the army that entertains the troops. That way, Elvis could give concerts at a few military bases, do some television commercials for the army, and have a pretty easy time of it. But neither the Colonel nor Elvis would hear of it. Instead, Elvis was sent to Fort Hood in Texas for basic training.

While Elvis was at Fort Hood, he and the Colonel discovered an army regulation that allowed military personnel to live off the post if they had dependents in the area. This regulation was originally intended to allow army personnel to live with their wives and children, but

Elvis had something else in mind. He moved his parents down to Texas and, claiming they were dependents (which, technically, they were), moved in with them.

Although she had never been very healthy, Gladys was doing particularly poorly during the summer of 1958. Elvis wanted to be with her, but her condition grew worse. On Friday, August 8, Elvis drove her to the train so she could return to Memphis and the family doctor.

When Gladys arrived in Memphis, she was hospitalized immediately. The diagnosis was hepatitis, which is a serious infection of the liver. Three days later, the doctors called Elvis. Obtaining an emergency leave, he flew up to Memphis Tuesday night. All through that night and the next day, Elvis and Vernon took turns sitting by Gladys's bedside. She died at three in the morning on Thursday. Elvis nearly collapsed at the funeral. "She was the sunshine of our home," he choked. "Goodbye, darling. . . . I love you so much. I lived my whole life just for you."[2]

During the next month, Elvis completed his training at Fort Hood, and then on September 19 shipped out to West Germany. He had announced earlier that Vernon and his grandmother, Minnie Mae Presley, would soon follow him there. "One of the last things Mom said was that Dad and I should always be together," Elvis told reporters. "Wherever they send me, Dad will go too."[3]

When Elvis's transport ship docked at Bremerhaven on October 1, there were five hundred screaming teenagers waiting on the dock. But it was the last they would see of the King of Rock and Roll for more than a year—unless they went to see one of his double features, that is.

Elvis was the model, crew-cut soldier. He always did what he was told and never complained, which was exactly the kind of behavior the Colonel needed to establish Elvis's new image. When it was announced some months later that Elvis would probably not let his famous sideburns grow back after his discharge, America's parents were reassured. The 23-year-old Elvis wasn't a monster at all, they realized. He'd just been kidding about all this rock and roll nonsense.

Elvis's first movie after his discharge from the army confirmed everything. Released in October 1960, *G.I. Blues* displayed the new Elvis: a ladies' man, sure, but also someone you could trust never to take advantage of anyone. In *G.I. Blues*, Elvis showed he was a rebel and outcast no longer. Colonel Tom couldn't have been happier. Rock and roll fans couldn't have been more depressed.

The last year had been a tough one. Three of rock and roll's biggest stars—Buddy Holly, Ritchie Valens, and the Big Bopper—were killed in a plane crash outside Fargo, North Dakota, while touring the Midwest. Chuck Berry was arrested for a violation of the Mann Act—specifically, transporting minors across state lines for immoral purposes. And Jerry Lee Lewis married his 13-year-old cousin, Myra, which caused such a righteous stir that the Killer was thrown off the radio. (Ironically, it turned out to be the longest of Jerry Lee's marriages, lasting thirteen years.)

Little Richard, too, gave it up. During a summer tour of Australia, on a flight to Sydney, one of his plane's engines caught fire. On the way down, Richard later claimed, he promised the Lord that if delivered safely, he would quit rock and roll and go back to the church. When the plane landed safely, Richard took off $20,000 worth of rings and tossed them into the sea. Then he went back to America, gave up rock and roll, and enrolled in Oakwood College, a Bible school in Huntsville, Alabama. After that, Richard played gospel revivals for almost ten years before returning to rock and roll in the mid-sixties.

With the biggest rock and roll stars of the fifties either dead or neutralized, the music seemed to lose its soul. Record companies used Elvis clones for a while—such as Frankie Avalon and Fabian—but their cottony-soft imitations only made the truth clearer: Rock and roll was dead.

Or was it just sleeping? When the Beatles landed in New York on February 7, 1964, John, Paul, George, and Ringo brought a surprise with them, a blast from the past. In America, the music had nearly been forgotten, but in England rock and roll was bigger than ever. "It was the black music we dug," John Lennon told *Rolling Stone* in 1971, but "when we came over here . . . nobody here was listening to rock and roll or to black music . . . We felt as though we were coming to the land of its origin, but nobody wanted to know about it."[4]

They were wrong: Everybody wanted to know about it. "I Want to Hold Your Hand" was the Beatles' first Number One single in America. The song entered the charts on January 18, 1964, at Number 45. The next week it was Number Three. On Febuary 1, it was Number One. During the next six days, "I Want to Hold Your Hand" sold more than 1.5 million copies.

It was like Elvis all over again: the screaming girls, the unprecedented record sales, and even a record

The Beatles on the Ed Sullivan show.

audience for Ed Sullivan the night the Beatles performed. Americans needed a relief after the ordeal of the assassination, and the Mop Tops gave it to them. The Beatles were *fun*, and they knew how to rock and roll.

While rock and roll was being reborn in new forms, however, Elvis stayed in Hollywood making movies. His 1964 and 1965 releases were *Kissin' Cousins, Viva Las Vegas, Roustabout, Girl Happy, Tickle Me,* and *Harum Scarum.* In *Harum Scarum,* for which the Colonel had masterfully negotiated a $1 million fee plus a cut of the profits, Elvis played a rock and roll singer who travels to an imaginary Mideast kingdom, is kidnapped by an evil band of assassins, escapes, falls in love with a princess, is recaptured, escapes again, and saves the kingdom from the king's evil brother. He gets the girl in the end, too.

8

The Hillbilly Cat Comes Back

During the sixties, the Beatles remade rock and roll along with some help from the Rolling Stones, the Jefferson Airplane, Bob Dylan, and many others. In the process, the music became identified with much more than a subculture. What developed instead during the sixties was an alternate culture, an oppositional culture, a counterculture. The sixties counterculture involved a lot more than music. It was concerned with protests against social injustice and the Vietnam War and with new ways of living and working. But, along with changes in dress and lifestyle, music was an important part of it.

But Elvis Presley, the man who started rock and roll, was not part of it. Instead, Elvis had cleaned up—in both senses. After the army, the sideburns had stayed off, as promised, and the fees had gone up—way up. In 1965, Elvis's income looked something like this:

- salary for *Paradise, Hawaiian Style*: $350,000
- salary for *Frankie and Johnny*: $650,000
- percentage of profits from *Tickle Me*: $850,000
- percentage of profits from *Girl Happy*: $850,000
- salary for *Harum Scarum*: $1,000,000
- record royalties: $1,125,000

Add in the licensing income from all the Elvis Presley merchandise and you get more than $5 million for that single year. It was a typical figure for Elvis in those years, and not a penny came from performing in public.

The King had made what seemed to be his last public appearance in March of 1961, at a benefit for a memorial to the U.S.S. *Arizona*, a battleship sunk in Pearl Harbor by Japanese bombers in 1941. Like the Beatles' last concert in San Francisco in 1966, the U.S.S. *Arizona* benefit hadn't been planned as a farewell performance; it just worked out that way.

In 1967, Elvis got married. His bride was Priscilla Beaulieu, the daughter of an army colonel. Elvis had met Priscilla while he was stationed in Germany. Priscilla was 14 when she met Elvis, and 21 when she married him.

Elvis seemed happy, but even as he continued to cash in on his movie soundtracks, the music passed him by. He was isolated, whether on a Hollywood sound stage or at Graceland, and he began to ask himself questions. Sitting in his Graceland jungle room with the astroturf on the ceiling or in the den with the three television sets—one for each network, just like the president had—Elvis wondered: Did he still have it? Would a live audience still respond to him? Could he still rock and roll?

In 1968, he finally got the opportunity to answer those questions. Because Elvis's popularity had recently been slipping at the box office, Colonel Parker had made a new kind of deal with NBC to keep his fee at the million-dollar mark. The deal called for both a movie and a TV special. The television show would be broadcast during Christmas 1968. Its producer and director would be Steve Binder.

"I felt very, very strongly that the television special was Elvis's moment of truth," Binder recalled. "If he did another MGM movie on the special, he would wipe out his career and he would be known only as that phenomenon who came along in the fifties, shook his hips, and had a great manager. On the reverse side, if he could do a special and prove he was still Number One, he could have a whole rejuvenation."[1]

What Binder wanted to do was bring Elvis back to his old days at Sun, before the Colonel took over, when Elvis made the music that Elvis wanted to make, because he liked it and for the kicks. The Colonel wanted Elvis to come out, sing Christmas songs, and say something like "Thank you very much, ladies and gentlemen. Merry Christmas and goodnight." The battle lines were drawn; it was up to Elvis to decide.

For once, Steve Binder outfoxed the Colonel. One day at a rehearsal, Binder asked Elvis what would happen if they walked out onto the street. Elvis seemed a bit nervous. He assumed he'd be mobbed by fans as he always had. But Binder coaxed him to find out.

"So we did it," Binder remembered. "Four o'clock in the afternoon and there we were. . . . We stood there to the point of embarassment. Kids were bumping into us and saying 'excuse me' or not even saying that. Elvis started talking louder than normal, trying to be recognized or noticed or something. But nothing happened. Nothing. Zero."[2]

Elvis was convinced. Something had to be done. Steve Binder was given a much freer hand. What he came up with, Elvis's first public performance in nearly eight years, has since become known as the Comeback Special.

It opened with a tight close-up of Elvis's face. Singing "Trouble," he looked it. His eyes were narrowed and he stood tough, as though he were considering whether or not to break someone's face. Soon, the camera pulled back and showed—oh-my-God, Elvis was wearing a black leather suit. And the sideburns . . . they were *back*.

Then the camera pulled even farther back and, all of a sudden, Elvis was right in the middle of a production number lifted directly out of his 1957 film *Jailhouse Rock*. The song was a new one, "Guitar Man," but it sounded old. The guitar went chunka- chunka-chunka. The drums went BOOM BOOM BOOM. Elvis looked cool.

A commercial break followed, and then Elvis was back again—sitting on a small stage this time, hanging out with most of his old gang from Sun: Scotty Moore, D. J. Fontana, and guiatarist Charlie Hodge.

The first song they did was "Lawdy Miss Clawdy," an ancient R & B number that Lloyd Price had made into a hit back in 1952 and Elvis had recorded in 1956 for RCA. Twelve years later, it hadn't aged at all. Maybe it was even better. Elvis really belted it out, gutting it the way Jerry Lee Lewis or Little Richard would have, singing as he hadn't sung since he was poor.

Between songs, Elvis joked around with the boys, not minding the audience at all. At one point, he started to sneer but then stopped himself. "Wait a minute," he said. "There's something wrong with my lip."[3]

Then he stood up to do "Heartbreak Hotel." A few years earlier he had put on some extra weight, but now he was thin again, lean and hard as he had been at 21 when he first destroyed audiences with this song. The knee bent, the leg shook, the hips wiggled, and you could see why the girls had always gone wild. The music hadn't left Elvis behind.

The highlight of the show was "That's All Right Mama," with Scotty Moore reprising his famous guitar part. It sounded just as fresh and alive as it had the day they recorded it—July 6, 1954—more than fourteen years before. "I really like a lot of the new music," Elvis told the audience, "but rock and roll music is basically gospel and rhythm and blues, or it sprang from that."[4] Then he sang a gospel number called "Where Could I Go But to the Lord?"

There were some awkward moments, of course, but Elvis nevertheless proved that he was still ELVIS, as one of the show's sets screamed in letters twenty feet high.

The comeback special.

A rush of singles—mostly ballads, rather than fast rock songs—followed and put Elvis back on top of the charts. "In the Ghetto," "Don't Cry, Daddy," "The Wonder of You"—all made it into the Top Ten. "Suspicious Minds" even climbed all the way to Number One. Elvis started touring again. He was particularly popular with middle-aged audiences in Las Vegas, crowds of fifties teenagers now grown up.

After the Christmas special, Elvis asked Steve Binder what he thought the future might hold. "Elvis," Binder told him, "my real, real feeling is that I don't know if you'll do any [of the] great things you want to do. Maybe the bed has been made already, maybe this'll be just a little fresh air you'll experience for a month."

"No, no, I won't," Elvis said. "I'm going to do things."[5] But Binder was right. Although the fresh air lasted longer than a month, the bed had already been made.

Fans flocked to see Elvis, who regularly sold out stadiums and sports arenas. He was making $200,000 a week in Las Vegas whenever he felt like it. But while the halls were full, Elvis's life was empty.

His marriage to Priscilla ended on October 9, 1973, just five years after the birth of their only daughter, Lisa Marie. Elvis was already having difficulties dealing with his increasing age; the divorce merely led to more prolonged bouts of emotional instability. As a result, Elvis became dependent on drugs—drugs to wake up, drugs to go to sleep, drugs to give him the energy to perform, and drugs to control his nerves and his appetite.

For all the older fans who wanted to remember the dangerous days of their youth, Elvis was as satisfying as nostalgia could be. As the *Milwaukee Journal* reported, "The audiences at those concerts were something to behold, so adoring were they. Elvis would come on, overweight but regally commanding, and thousands of cameras would light up like rippling waves of fireflies wherever he turned."[6]

For Elvis, though, remembering the success of his youth was painful because it only called attention to all that he had lost. He had mattered once, and now he seemed to be just a curiosity. Every day, he became more and more like a freak in one of the Colonel's old circus sideshows. The money was still pouring in by the planeload, but Elvis had money enough. What he didn't have was respect.

Onstage, Elvis wore ridiculously flashy jeweled costumes. He went through all his old moves, and even added an entire set of new ones, including karate kicks and scarf tosses. But the effort to recapture his youth only made things worse and more farcical.

For rock and rollers to make themselves over, they've got to believe in the image. It has to feel real to them or it won't be real to anyone else. The night of the Comeback Special, Elvis believed. Afterward, he wasn't so sure.

He was so many things to so many people—a rocker, a mama's boy, a dutiful soldier, a movie star, a recluse—that he lost track of himself. Pleasing people was both his talent and his curse. "He could be all things to all people," Greil Marcus wrote, "but his eagerness to prove it . . . destroyed his ability to focus his talent."[7]

Elvis continued to drift. As the years passed, he let other people do his thinking for him. In business matters, Colonel Parker had complete say—Elvis began to see even less of the fabulous sums he was earning. As far as his personal life was concerned, he rarely left the company of the Memphis Mafia, spending all his time with Red and Sonny West, two friends from his high school days at Humes, and the rest of his gang of bodyguards and professional friends. Elvis's road manager, Joe Esposito, took care of anything that needed to be done.

The downside of his regained popularity was that he couldn't go out in public without being recognized. Elvis wasn't about to cause any more riots, but he used this as an excuse to keep to himself, secure behind the safe stone walls of Graceland.

Elvis avoided other people in his last years. If he wanted to go out someplace, like an amusement park, he would just have Esposito rent the whole place after hours. Usually this was very late at night, but Elvis didn't mind. He wasn't sleeping too well, anyway.

Elvis meets President Richard Nixon.

Elvis in his rhinestone period.

9

Long Live the King

At first light in Memphis, August 16, 1977, seemed to be a routine midsummer Tuesday. The weather was typically hot, sunny, and humid, and the forecast was for more of the same. Elvis Presley had been up all night, but that wasn't unusual, either.

Sometime late Monday night or very early Tuesday morning Elvis had decided to visit his dentist. After that, he had returned to Graceland and played racquetball with his cousin, Billy Smith. Elvis had built a racquetball court out back, and while he and Billy played, Billy's wife and Ginger Alden watched from the luxurious lounge. Elvis was dating Ginger, a 20-year-old Memphis beauty queen. Later, Ginger would say that she and Elvis had agreed that night to be married on Christmas Day.

The racquetball game went on from 4:00 A.M. until about 5:30 A.M., when Elvis and Ginger went to bed. Elvis took some pills to help him sleep. Elvis was taking a lot of pills, and they were affecting him both emotionally and physically. At 19, Elvis had been a lean 175 pounds, but now the pills and overeating had bloated him to well over 200 pounds.

"Sometimes I couldn't believe it," Sonny West told a reporter at the time, "Elvis would be sitting there, his eyes closed, his head hanging down, his mouth open— and he couldn't even manage to get his eyes open. He was on pills all day long, and he would give himself shots in the arm or the leg with those little plastic syringes. He would have us give him shots in the rear end. We prayed for this man many times."[1]

The pills were generally prescribed for Elvis by his personal physician, Dr. George Nichopoulos.

At about 8:00 A.M., Ginger was awakened by Elvis, who was calling down for some more pills because he still couldn't sleep. Elvis picked up a book and went into his combination sitting room-bathroom to read for a while.

Ginger woke up again just after 2:00 P.M. It was even hotter outside. She called for Elvis, but there was no answer. She went into the bathroom. She saw Elvis was lying on the floor, face down, not moving.

"I slapped him a few times," Ginger told the *Memphis Commercial Appeal*. "It was like he breathed once when I turned his head. I raised one of his eyes and it was blood red, but I couldn't move him."[2]

Immediately, she called down to Joe Esposito. Esposito called Dr. Nichopoulos. At first, they tried mouth-to-mouth resuscitation. Then the ambulance came, and the paramedics took over. "Come on, Presley, breathe! Breathe for me!" Nichopoulos urged as the ambulance sped to the hospital.[3]

It was no use. Elvis Presley was dead at 42. Later, the coroner said he believed Elvis had been dead since around nine o'clock that morning.

He was one of the most famous men in the world, adored by millions of fans and wealthy beyond imagination. But the pressure of that fame proved to be too much for Elvis Presley. It was not something that a young man from Tupelo, Mississippi, could ever have been prepared for. Drugs had helped him to relieve the pressure. But Elvis paid for that relief with his life.

In its obituary, *The Times* of London called Elvis "the catalyst of the still unabated youth revolution."[4] It was a revolution that began shortly after World War II.

The postwar boom created teenagers as we know them today. The teenagers changed American society. Elvis was only the beginning. Throughout the sixties, a decade of great social upheaval, America's young people made it abundantly clear that they intended to have a substantial say in the nation's culture and politics. Rock and roll didn't lead directly to political activity, but the music did give young people a sense of themselves, as individuals and as a generation, that separated them from the world of their parents.

Right from the start, teenagers understood what the BOOM BOOM BOOM of the drums meant. In the words of rock historian Greil Marcus, it was all about "the sense of being caught up in something much bigger than your own personal taste."[5] Rock and roll was fun. It also seemed historic.

As a result, some people have claimed that Elvis was just lucky. They argue that he just happened to be in the right place at the right time—that historical forces, not Elvis, created and explain rock and roll. But the first superstar of the television age deserves a bit more credit.

Elvis, of course, knew a good thing when he saw it, and he ran with it. But if there were so many Elvises waiting to be discovered, why couldn't Sam Phillips find another one? There is a logic to be found in the rise of rock and roll. Elvis's phenomenally rapid success proved that an audience had been waiting for him, and historical arguments about postwar teenagers help illuminate the subject. But in the process, Elvis's talent is too often lost.

He wasn't a very good guitar player. He didn't even write his own songs. But Elvis did understand what rock and roll had to be as few others could have.

Because of his unique background, Elvis personified the tensions that gave rock and roll its dynamic power and its bite. His gospel and country roots, the poor childhood that exposed him to the southern black subculture, his love for his mother—all these traits were then filtered through Elvis's urban Memphis adolescence, and what came out was a mix that was unprecedented in American popular culture.

Elvis was at once everything and nothing, as big as America and as hard to pin down. Eventually, his fame swallowed him up. But not before he gave the world rock and roll.

Important Events in Elvis Presley's Life

1935	Born January 8 in East Tupelo, Mississippi.
1945	Wins second prize at the Mississippi-Alabama Fair talent show, singing "Old Shep."
1948	Moves with family to Memphis; enters L. C. Humes High School.
1953	Visits Sam Phillips's Memphis Recording Service for the first time.
1954	Makes first record for Sun with Scotty Moore and Bill Black.
1955	Accepts Colonel Tom Parker's offer of managerial help in February; Parker arranges the sale of his contract to RCA Victor in November.
1956	Records "Heartbreak Hotel" in January; the song tops the charts on April 21.
	Appears in front of 54 million people on Ed Sullivan's "Toast of the Town" on September 9.
	Love Me Tender is released in November.
1957	Drafted December 20.
1961	Performs in March at a benefit for a memorial to the U.S.S. *Arizona,* his last public appearance for nearly eight years.
1967	Marries Priscilla Beaulieu.
1968	Daughter Lisa Marie is born.
	Makes comeback on NBC Christmas special.
1973	Divorces Priscilla on October 9.
1977	Dies at Graceland on August 16.

Notes

Chapter 1

1 *Milwaukee Journal*, August 17, 1977.
2 *Washington Post*, August 17, 1977.
3 *Times* (London), August 18, 1977.
4 *New York Times*, August 18, 1977.
5 *New York Times*, August 18, 1977.
6 *New York Times*, August 19, 1977.
7 *Denver Post*, August 18, 1977.

Chapter 2

1 Greil Marcus, *Mystery Train* (New York: Dutton, 1982) p . 150.
2 Jerry Hopkins, *Elvis* (New York: Simon and Schuster, 1971), p. 19.
3 Hopkins, p. 25.
4 Hopkins, p. 24.
5 Nik Cohn, *Rock from the Beginning* (New York: Pocket, 1970), p. 13.
6 Hopkins, p. 27.
7 Hopkins, p. 27.
8 Hopkins, p. 28.
9 Marcus, p. 152-53.
10 Lawrence N. Redd, *Rock Is Rhythm and Blues* (Lansing: Michigan State University Press, 1974), p. 134.
11 Charlie Gillett, *Sound of the City* (New York: Dell, 1972), p. 39.
12 Hopkins, p. 31.
13 Hopkins, p. 32.

Chapter 3

1 Hopkins, p. 46.
2 Peter Guralnick in Jim Miller, ed., *Rolling Stone History of Rock & Roll* (New York: Random House/Rolling Stone Press, 1976), p. 33.
3 Marcus, p. 159.
4 Hopkins, pp. 39-40.

Chapter 4

1 Hopkins, p. 65.
2 Hopkins, p. 62.
3 Hopkins, p. 64.
4 Hopkins, p. 68.
5 Hopkins, p. 69.
6 Hopkins, p. 69.
7 Marcus, p. 178.
8 Hopkins, p. 72.
9 Hopkins, p. 72.
10 Hopkins, p. 73.
11 *Elvis: The Sun Sessions* (RCA Records), liner notes.
12 Hopkins, p. 74.
13 Gillett, p. 34.
14 Guralnick in Miller ed., p. 30.

Chapter 5

1 Guralnick in Miller ed., p. 30.

2 Hopkins, p. 77.
3 Hopkins, p. 79.
4 Hopkins, p. 82.

Chapter 6

1 *New York Post*, August 17, 1977.
2 Cohn, p. 12.
3 Steve Chapple and Reebee Garofalo, *Rock 'n' Roll is Here to Pay* (Chicago: Nelson Hall, 1977), p. 43.
4 *Washington Post*, August 17, 1977.
5 *Washington Post*, August 17, 1977.
6 Chapple and Garofalo, p. 46.
7 Marcus, p. 169.
8 Michael Lydon, *Rock Folk* (New York: Dial, 1971), p. 10.
9 Mike Daly in Greil Marcus ed., *Rock and Roll Will Stand* (Boston: Beacon, 1969), p. 30.
10 Langdon Winner in Miller, ed., p. 52.
11 *The Rolling Stone Interviews: 1967-1980* (New York: St. Martin's/Rolling Stone Press, 1981), p. 91.
12 *New York Times*, August 17, 1977.
13 *New York Times*, August 17, 1977.
14 *New York Times*, August 17, 1977.

Chapter 7

1 Hopkins, p. 206.
2 Cohn, p. 163.
3 Hopkins, p. 217.
4 Cohn, p. 65
5 Chapple and Garofalo, p. 51.
6 *Interviews with Phil Ochs* (Folkways Records).
7 *The Rolling Stone Interviews*, p. 148
8 Anthony Scaduto, Bob Dylan (New York: New American Library, 1973, p. 203-4.
9 Scaduto, p. 204.

Chapter 8

1 Hopkins, p. 335.
2 Hopkins, p. 338-39.
3 Elvis: '68 Comeback Special (Music Media video).
4 Elvis: '68 Comeback Special.
5 Hopkins, p. 345.
6 *Milwaukee Journal*, August 17, 1977.
7 Marcus, p. 189-90.

Chapter 9

1 *St. Louis Post Dispatch*, August 17, 1977.
2 New York Post, August 17, 1977.
3 *Milwaukee Journal*, August 17, 1977.
4 *Times* (London), August 18, 1977.
5 Greil Marcus in Miller, ed., p. 174.

Suggested Reading

ELVIS PRESLEY

Dundy, Elaine. *Elvis and Gladys*. New York: Macmillan, 1985.

Hopkins, Jerry. *Elvis: The Final Years*. New York: St. Martin's, 1980.

Marsh, Dave. *Elvis*. New York: Times Books/Rolling Stone Press, 1982.

Presley, Priscilla Beaulieu, with Sandra Harmon. *Elvis and Me*. New York: St. Martin's, 1985.

ROCK AND ROLL

Christgau, Robert. *Any Old Way You Choose It*. Baltimore: Penguin, 1973.

Davies, Hunter. *The Beatles*. New York: McGraw-Hill, 1968.

Denisoff, R. Serge. *Great Day Coming: Folk Music and the American Left*. Urbana: University of Illinois Press, 1971.

Frith, Simon. *Sound Effects*. New York: Pantheon, 1981.

Guralnick, Peter. *Lost Highway*. Boston: Godine, 1979.

Palmer, Robert. *Deep Blues*. New York: Viking, 1971.

Stambler, Irwin. *Encyclopedia of Pop, Rock & Soul*. New York: St. Martin's, 1977.

Whitburn, Joel. *The Billboard Book of Top 40 Hits*. New York: Billboard, 1983.

Index